Sydney George Lushington

County Electors Act, 1888

With Notes on the Changes Made in the Law of Parliamentary...

Sydney George Lushington

County Electors Act, 1888
With Notes on the Changes Made in the Law of Parliamentary...

ISBN/EAN: 9783337112257

Printed in Europe, USA, Canada, Australia, Japan

Cover: Foto ©Suzi / pixelio.de

More available books at **www.hansebooks.com**

THE

County Electors Act, 1888:

WITH NOTES ON THE CHANGES MADE IN THE LAW OF PARLIAMENTARY AND MUNICIPAL REGISTRATION, FOR THE PURPOSE OF FORMING A REGISTER OF PERSONS QUALIFIED TO VOTE AT ELECTIONS OF COUNTY AND DISTRICT COUNCILLORS,

AND

A CALENDAR OF OPERATIONS FOR THE CURRENT YEAR.

BEING

A Practical Guide to all concerned in the Registration of Parliamentary and Local Government Voters.

BY

S. G. LUSHINGTON, M.A., B.C.L.,

Of the Inner Temple, Barrister-at-Law.

LONDON:

SHAW & SONS, FETTER LANE & CRANE COURT, E.C.,

Law Printers and Publishers.

1888.

PREFACE.

THE object of this Edition of the County Electors Act, 1888, is to provide Clerks of the Peace, Town Clerks, Overseers, and Registration Agents with a complete view of the effect of the Act upon their respective duties relating to registration, especially in the present year.

The Act introduces much that is new in substance under the guise of old forms, and incorporates, by reference, much well-known law relating to the qualification and registration of burgesses for the purpose of applying it to the qualification and registration of the new county electors. A great part, therefore, of the notes consists in the citation of those enactments relating to burgesses, in full, but with the modifications necessary for applying them to county electors. This has been a laborious, but, it is hoped, an accurate and exhaustive method of arriving at the true effect of the Act.

A calendar of things to be done in order of date for the present year is prefixed to the body of the work.

The Index of Cases contains references to all the reports of each case cited so far as known to the Author.

S. G. L.

INNER TEMPLE,
16th May, 1888.

TABLE OF CASES.

A CALENDAR

OF THINGS TO BE DONE IN ORDER OF DATE IN THE YEAR 1888 UNDER

THE COUNTY ELECTORS ACT, 1888.

Clerks of the Peace and Town Clerks immediately to issue SUPPLEMENTAL Precepts and Forms.

June 20.—Overseers to publish notices that non-payment before the 20th July of poor rates made during the twelve months immediately preceding the 5th January last will disqualify parliamentary ten pounds occupiers and householders, also burgesses and county electors.

Notices should state that non-payment of assessed taxes will disqualify ten pounds occupiers for local government franchise and for parliamentary occupation franchise in parliamentary boroughs; and non-payment of county rates will disqualify burgess occupiers under section 2 in counties, and non-payment of borough rates will disqualify burgesses not being ten pounds occupiers under section 3.

June 20.—Serve notices as to non-payment where rates have not been previously duly demanded.

July 20.—Last day for payment of rates, and in counties last day for claims as parliamentary ownership voters.

July 22.—Second return of deaths is now due to overseers from registrars of births and deaths.

List of defaulters in payment of assessed taxes is now due to overseers from collectors of taxes.

Overseers to make out list of persons disqualified for non-payment of rates, and to keep it open for inspection for fourteen days, and deliver copies on payment of fees.

July 25.—Last day for old lodgers' claims. In counties, overseers to remove published copy ownership portion of parliamentary register, and notice to send in parliamentary ownership claims.

July 31.—Overseers to ascertain from relieving officer names of persons disqualified by receipt of parochial relief.

July 31.—Overseers in counties to make out occupiers' and supplemental occupiers' lists and separate lists of non-residents qualified to be county councillors, and lists of parliamentary ownership claimants and old lodgers with marginal objections.

Overseers in boroughs to make out occupiers' list in divisions, old lodgers' list with marginal objections, reserved rights' list, if any, aldermen and councillors' list, and parish burgess lists.

August 1.—Overseers to sign, publish, keep for inspection, and on payment of fees deliver copies of all the above lists.

Aug. 20.—Last day for notices of objection and for occupiers' and new lodgers' claims.

Aug. 25.—Overseers to make out claim and objection lists, viz.:—

General list of claimants both as parliamentary occupation voters (other than lodgers) and as county electors or burgesses.

List of claimants as parliamentary occupation voters (other than lodgers), but not as county electors or burgesses.

Aug. 25.—List of claimants as county electors or burgesses only.

List of claimants as new lodgers.

List of claims to be on the separate non-resident list of persons qualified to be county councillors, but not county electors or burgesses.

List of claims, in boroughs, to be on the separate non-resident list of persons qualified to be aldermen or borough councillors, but not burgesses.

List of persons objected to, in counties, as parliamentary ownership voters.

List of persons objected to, both as parliamentary occupation voters (other than lodgers) and as county electors or burgesses.

List of persons objected to as parliamentary occupation voters (other than lodgers) but not objected to as county electors or burgesses.

List of persons objected to as county electors or burgesses only.

List of persons objected to as on the separate non-resident list of persons qualified to be county councillors, but not to be county electors or burgesses.

Aug. 25.—List of persons objected to in boroughs as on the separate non-resident aldermen and borough councillors' list.

List of persons objected to as on the old lodgers' list.

Overseers to sign, publish, keep for inspection, and on payment of fees deliver copies of all these claim and objection lists.

Overseers in municipal boroughs to send to the clerk of the peace for the county, and to the town clerk—

(*a*) Two copies of the occupiers' and old lodgers' lists ; and

(*b*) A copy of each of the occupiers' and lodgers' claim and objection lists.

And if such municipal borough is not in a parliamentary borough, send also to the clerk of the peace—

(*a*) The list of parliamentary ownership claimants ;

(*b*) Copy ownership portion of parliamentary register, with marginal additions ;

(*c*) Copy list of parliamentary ownership voters objected to.

Aug. 25.—But if such borough is in a parliamentary or merged parliamentary borough, send also to the town clerk two copies of the reserved rights' list, if any.

Overseers in counties but not in boroughs to send to the clerk of the peace—

(*a*) The list of parliamentary ownership claimants.

(*b*) Copy ownership portion of parliamentary register, with marginal additions.

(*c*) Copy list of parliamentary ownership voters objected to.

(*d*) Two copies of the occupiers' and supplemental occupiers' and old lodgers' lists ; and

(*e*) A copy of each of the occupiers' and lodgers' claim and objection lists.

Sept. 5.—Last day for sending in declarations of change of abode to clerks of the peace, and declarations as to misdescription to town clerks.

Sept. 8.—First day for holding revision courts.

Oct. 27.—Last day for entering notices of appeal at Central Office, Royal Courts of Justice, Strand.

Oct. 28.—First day for hearing appeals from revising barristers.

Oct. 31.—Last day for holding revising barristers' courts.

THE COUNTY ELECTORS ACT, 1888
51 VICT. c. 10.

AN ACT to provide for the Qualification and Registration of Electors for the purposes of Local Government in England and Wales.
[16th May, 1888.]

WHEREAS it is expedient to make provision with respect to the qualification and registration of electors of any representative bodies (in this Act referred to as "county authorities") which may be established under any Act of the present session of Parliament for the purposes of local government in counties in England:

Be it therefore enacted by the Queen's most Excellent Majesty, by and with the advice and consent of the Lords Spiritual and Temporal, and Commons, in this present Parliament assembled, and by the authority of the same, as follows:

[The representative bodies here referred to are the county and district councils intended to be established for the purposes of local government under the Local Government Bill now under the consideration of Parliament.]

1. This Act may be cited as the County Electors Act, 1888. *Short title and construction*

The Registration Act, 1885, and the Parliamentary Registration Acts within the meaning of that *48 & 49 Vict. c. 15.*

Sect. 1. Act, are in this Act referred to as the Registration of Electors Acts, and together with this Act may be cited as the Registration of Electors Acts, 1843 to 1888.

This Act shall be construed as one with the Registration of Electors Acts.

"The Parliamentary Registration Acts."

By the nineteenth section of the Registration Act, 1885 (48 Vict. c. 15), the expression "Parliamentary Registration Acts" means the Parliamentary Registration Act, 1843 (6 & 7 Vict. c. 18), and the Parliamentary and Municipal Registration Act, 1878 (41 & 42 Vict. c. 26), inclusive of any Acts and enactments amending the said Acts, or otherwise relating to revising barristers or to the registration of voters, and of any Acts or enactments relating to rating so far as they are auxiliary to or deal with the registration of voters.

"The Registration of Electors Acts."

The following Acts and enactments, therefore, are in this Act included in the expression the Registration of Electors Acts:—

The Parliamentary Registration Act, 1843, 6 & 7 Vict. c. 18.

An Act relating to Payment of Rates and Taxes, 1848, 11 & 12 Vict. c. 90.

Compound Householders Act, 1851, 14 & 15 Vict. c. 14.

County Voters Registration Act, 1865, 28 Vict. c. 36.

Revising Barristers Act, 1866, 29 & 30 Vict. c. 54.

Vaccination Act, 1867, 30 & 31 Vict. c. 84, s. 26.

Representation of the People Act, 1867, 30 & 31 Vict. c. 102.

Parliamentary Electors Registration Act, 1868, 31 & 32 Vict. c. 58.

Revenue Officers Disabilities Removal Act, 1868, 31 & 32 Vict. c. 73.

Customs and Inland Revenue Duties Act, 1869, 32 & 33 Vict. c. 14, s. 8.

Poor Rate Assessment and Collection Act, 1869, 32 & 33 Vict. c. 41. **Notes to Sect. 1.**

Elementary Education Act, 1870, 33 & 34 Vict. c. 75, s. 91.

Parliamentary and Municipal Elections Act, 1872, 35 & 36 Vict. c. 33.

Revising Barristers Act, 1873, 36 & 37 Vict. c. 70.

Revenue Officers Disabilities Removal Act, 1874, 37 & 38 Vict. c. 22.

Revising Barristers Act, 1874, 37 & 38 Vict. c. 53.

Rating Act, 1874, 37 & 38 Vict. c. 54.

Elementary Education Act, 1876, 39 & 40 Vict. c. 79, s. 10.

House Occupiers Disqualification Removal Act, 1878, 41 Vict. c. 3.

Parliamentary and Municipal Registration Act, 1878, 41 & 42 Vict. c. 26.

Assessed Rates Act, 1879, 42 Vict. c. 10.

Supreme Court of Judicature Act, 1881, 44 & 45 Vict. c. 68, s. 14.

Municipal Corporations Act, 1882, 45 & 46 Vict. c. 50.

Diseases Prevention (Metropolis) Act, 1883, 46 & 47 Vict. c. 35, s. 7.

Corrupt and Illegal Practices Prevention Act, 1883, 46 & 47 Vict. c. 51.

Municipal Elections (Corrupt and Illegal Practices) Act, 1884, 47 & 48 Vict. c. 70.

Representation of the People Act, 1884, 48 Vict. c. 3.

Municipal Voters Relief Act, 1885, 48 Vict. c. 9.

Registration Act, 1885, 48 Vict. c. 15.

Redistribution of Seats Act, 1885, 48 & 49 Vict. c. 23.

Medical Relief Disqualification Removal Act, 1885, 48 & 49 Vict. c. 46.

Revising Barristers Act, 1886, 49 & 50 Vict. c. 42.

Police Disabilities Removal Act, 50 Vict. sess. 2, c. 9.

Extension of burgess franchise to county

2.—(1.) For the purpose of the election of county authorities in England, the burgess quali-

Sect. 2. electors outside municipal boroughs 45 & 46 Vict. c. 50.

fication, that is to say, the qualification enacted by section nine of the Municipal Corporations Act, 1882, shall extend to every part of a county not within the limits of a borough, and a person possessing in any part of a county outside the limits of a borough such burgess qualification, shall be entitled to be registered under this Act as a county elector in the parish in which the qualifying property is situate.

(2.) Sections nine, thirty-one, thirty-three, and sixty-three of the Municipal Corporations Act, 1882, and any enactments of that or any other Act affecting the same, shall extend to so much of every county as is not comprised within the limits of a municipal borough in like manner as if they were herein re-enacted, with the substitution of "county" for "borough" and of "county elector" for "burgess," and with the other necessary modifications.

Meaning of "county" and "borough."

"Every part of a county not within the limits of a borough." "A county" means an area for which a separate county council is to be elected under the Local Government Bill, but does not include any borough made a county of itself for the purposes of that Bill. "A borough" includes every city or town to which the Municipal Corporations Act, 1882 (45 & 46 Vict. c. 50), applies, and also the city of London.

Boundary of county for first election.

The first council elected under the Local Government Bill for any county (save for the county of London or for any borough made a county of itself under the Act) is to be elected for the county as bounded at the passing of the

Notes to Sect. 2.

Act for the purpose of the election of members to serve in Parliament for the county, with this qualification, that where any urban sanitary district is situate partly within and partly without the boundary of such county, the district is to be deemed to be within that county which contains the largest portion of the population of the district according to the census of 1881. And if any difference arises as to the county which contains the largest portion of the population of any such district, such difference is to be referred to the Local Government Board, whose decision is to be final. (L. G. B., Part IV., s. 51.)

County of London.

The county of London under the Local Government Bill includes the city of London and the parishes and places in schedules A., B., and C. to the Metropolis Management Act, 1855 (18 & 19 Vict. c. 120).

Boroughs made counties of themselves.

Boroughs made counties of themselves under the Bill are Liverpool, Birmingham, Manchester, Leeds, Sheffield, Bristol, Bradford, Nottingham, Kingston-on-Hull, and Newcastle-on-Tyne. (L. G. B., sched. 4.) The Government have also agreed to add Salford, West Ham, Portsmouth, Leicester, Sunderland, Oldham, Brighton, Bolton, and Blackburn.

Private amendments further suggest the following ancient counties of cities and counties of towns, viz., York, Chester, Lincoln, Worcester, Gloucester, Exeter, Norwich, and Southampton, and also Cardiff, Burnley, Preston, Walsall, Derby, Northampton, Swansea, Rochdale, Croydon, St. Helen's, Huddersfield, Bath, Stockport, Wigan, Birkenhead, and Warrington.

Meaning of "parish."

"Parish in which the qualifying property is situate." At the common law a parish is said to be the place in which the congregation of any church is resident, but if a place has not a church, churchwardens, and sacramentalia, it is not properly a parish, though it has a district overseer and maintains its own poor, and also has a chapel warden by whom the rates are collected and paid to another parish. (Com. Dig. Tit. Parish, B.)

But in the Parliamentary and Municipal Registration Act, 1878 (41 & 42 Vict. c. 26, s. 4), the word "parish" is

Notes to Sect. 2.

defined as "a place for which a separate poor rate is or can be made, or for which a separate overseer is or can be appointed," and in the Municipal Corporations Act, 1882 (45 & 46 Vict. c. 50, s. 7), as "any place for which a separate poor rate is or can be made." In the other Parliamentary Registration Acts the word is not defined, or is used always in conjunction with the words "or township." In the Registration Act, 1885 (48 Vict. c. 15, s. 19), it is enacted that in this Act, unless the context otherwise requires, other expressions (after specifying certain expressions, not including the word "parish") have the same meaning as in the Parliamentary Registration Acts.

Divided parishes.

The expression "parish" in this sub-section and generally throughout the Act, where a parish is situate partly within and partly without the boundary of a parliamentary borough, or of a municipal borough, must be taken to include any part not within the boundary of such parliamentary or municipal borough, as if it were a separate parish (see section 9 of the Registration Act, 1885, 48 Vict. c. 15), and the overseers of the entire parish must act in each such part as if it were a separate parish.

Formerly, a number of places throughout England were extra-parochial, but at the common law there never was any place in England out of some county, though it might be extra-parochial. (Per Holt, C.J., Skinner's Rep. 685.)

Places formerly extra-parochial.

For these places provision was made by the twenty-second section of the Parliamentary Registration Act, 1843 (6 & 7 Vict. c. 18), as follows, viz.:—"Every precinct or place, whether extra-parochial or otherwise, which shall have no overseers of the poor shall, for the purposes of making any claim, and making out any list directed by this Act, be deemed to be within the parish or township adjoining thereto, and sharing in the right of election to which such claim or list may relate, and if such parish or place shall adjoin two or more parishes or townships as aforesaid, it shall be deemed to be within the least populous of such parishes or townships, according to the last census for the time being."

But although this enactment stands unrepealed, there

Notes to Sect. 2.

are now no such extra-parochial places, for by section one of the 20 Vict. c. 19, it is enacted that after the 31st day of December, 1857, every place entered separately in the report of the Registrar-General which then was, or was reputed to be extra-parochial, and wherein no rate was levied for the relief of the poor, shall for all purposes, including amongst others the registration of parliamentary and municipal voters, be deemed a parish for such purposes and designated by the name assigned to it in such report, and the justices having jurisdiction therein shall appoint overseers. And by section twenty-seven of the Poor Law Amendment Act, 1868 (31 & 32 Vict. 122), it was further enacted that from the 25th of December, 1868, every place which was or is reputed to be extra-parochial, whether entered by name in the report upon the census for the year 1851 or not, for which any overseer had not been then appointed or was not then acting, or which had not been then annexed to and incorporated with an adjoining parish, shall for all civil parochial purposes be annexed to and incorporated with the next adjoining parish with which it has the longest common boundary, and in case there shall be two or more parishes with which it shall have boundaries of equal extent, then with that parish which at the date of the passing of the Act contained the lowest amount of rateable value.

Meaning of "qualifying property."

"Qualifying property" is the expression used in the Municipal Corporations Act, 1882 (45 & 46 Vict. c. 50, s. 9), to denote any house, warehouse, counting-house, shop, or other building in respect of the occupation of which any person is entitled to be enrolled as a burgess, and so here in this Act it is used to denote any house, warehouse, counting-house, shop, or other building in respect of the occupation of which any person is under this Act entitled to be registered as a county elector.

Section 9 of the Municipal Corporations Act, 1882 (45 & 46 Vict. c. 50), as applied by this sub-section, will read as follows, viz.:—

Qualification of a county elector.

(1) A person shall not be deemed *a county elector* for any purpose unless he is registered as a *county elector*.

Notes to Sect. 2.

(2) A person shall not be entitled to be registered as a *county elector* unless he is qualified under section 3 of the County Electors Act, 1888, or as follows, viz.:

(*a*) Is of full age; and

(*b*) Is on the 15th July in any year, and has been during the whole of the then last preceding twelve months, in occupation, joint or several, of any house, warehouse, counting-house, shop, or other building (in this Act referred to as the qualifying property) in the *county;* and

(*c*) Has during the whole of those twelve months resided in the *county*, or within seven miles thereof; and

(*d*) Has been rated in respect of the qualifying property to all poor rates made during those twelve months for the parish wherein the property is situate; and

(*e*) Has on or before the twentieth of the same July paid all such rates, including *county* rates (if any), as have become payable by him in respect of the qualifying property up to the then last preceding fifth of January.

(3) Every person so qualified shall be entitled to be registered as a *county elector in the parish in which the qualifying property is situate*, unless he

(*a*) Is an alien; or

(*b*) Has within the twelve months aforesaid received union or parochial relief or other alms; or

(*c*) Is disentitled under any Act of Parliament.

With regard to this enactment it is to be noted that—

Full age.

A man attains his full age in law on the day before his twenty-first birthday, and the law in general takes no notice of fractions of a day, so that if a man is born on the first of January he is of full age on the morning of the thirty-first of December in the twenty-first year afterwards In order to entitle a person to be registered as a county elector, it is sufficient if he attains his full age of twenty-one years on the fifteenth of July in the year in which he is to be registered (*Powell* v. *Bradley* (1864), 18 C. B. (N.S.) 65); but it is not sufficient if he only attains his full age after that date, but before an election can take place. (*Hargreaves* v. *Hopper* (1875), 1 C. P. D. 195.)

Occupation by service.

An occupation by virtue of any office, service, or employment, that is to say, where a person is not merely *permitted* to occupy as a reward in the performance of his employer's contract to pay him, but *required* to occupy in the performance of his own contract to serve, is not sufficient to qualify for registration as a county elector. (*M'Clean* v. *Prichard* (1887), 20 Q. B. D. 285.)

Residence.

It is not very easy accurately to define what is a sufficient residence for the purposes of registration. The rule upon this subject may, however, perhaps be stated thus. That in order to constitute residence, a party must possess at the least a sleeping-apartment; but that an uninterrupted abiding at such dwelling is not requisite. If there be the liberty to return at any time (except as hereinafter noted with reference to the letting of a furnished house), and no abandonment (subject to that exception) of the intention to return whenever it may suit the party's pleasure or convenience to do so, a sufficient legal residence may be inferred. But if, save as aforesaid, a party by his own act or by the force of law is debarred from returning at any such time, he cannot be said to have even a constructive residence. As, for instance, if the party has contracted to give his personal services daily at such a distance from the qualifying property as practically to prevent his returning thereto without a breach of the contract during the term of the service (*Beal* v. *The Town Clerk of Exeter* (1887), 20 Q. B. D. 300); or if he were imprisoned during the qualifying period at a distance of more than seven miles from the county (*Powell* v. *Guest* (1864), 18 C. B. (N.S.) 72.)

Rating and payment of rates.

By the seventeenth section of the Poor Rate Assessment and Collection Act, 1869 (32 & 33 Vict. c. 41), a poor rate shall be deemed to be made on the day on which it is allowed by the justices, and if the justices sever in their allowance then on the day of their last allowance.

Notes to Sect. 2.

It is the bounden duty of the overseers to enter the name of the occupier of every rateable hereditament in the rate book in all cases whatsoever without regard to the person from whom the rate is collected, but if any name is entered in the rate book as that of the person rated in respect of the premises, it is a sufficient rating of the occupier for the purposes of his qualification as a county elector. (Poor Rate Assessment and Collection Act, 1869, 32 & 33 Vict. 41, s. 14 ; Parliamentary and Municipal Registration Act, 1878, 41 & 42 Vict. c. 26, s. 19.)

But if no name at all of any person whatever is entered in the rate book as that of a person rated in respect of the premises, then the occupier ought to make claim to be rated and tender payment of rates due as hereinafter mentioned.

A poor rate does not become payable unless it appears to be valid on the face of it, and there is nothing more to be done which the law requires to be done in order to bring home his liability to the party liable for the payment of it. For instance, a rate not signed by two justices as required by 43 Eliz. c. 2, is not valid on the face of it, and does not, therefore, become payable at any time. (*Fox* v. *Davies* (1848), 6 C. B. 11.) Or, if an outgoing tenant has not paid a rate, and the incoming tenant has never been called upon to make good his default, that rate is not one which has become payable from the incomer. (*Flatcher* v. *Boodle* (1865), 18 C. B. (N.S.) 152.)

The rates which must have been paid in order to entitle a person to be registered as a county elector include all sums due in respect of the qualifying property on account of any poor rate made and allowed, or any county rate made during the twelve months immediately preceding the 5th of January in the year of registration, and all such sums must have been paid on or before the twentieth of July in the same year.

County rates are assessed upon property rateable to the poor rate, and are levied under the 15 & 16 Vict. c. 52, and the Acts and enactments amending and affecting that Act, and in the great majority of parishes are levied together with the poor rates.

Notes to Sect. 2.

Payment of rates may be made on behalf of a voter, and will hold good for the purposes of his qualification if made for him by those whom he has procured to do so by giving them value for it, as payment by his landlord in consideration of higher rent. (*Wright* v. *Stockport* (1843), 5 M. & G. 33.) But excusal from payment on the ground of poverty is not equivalent to payment for the purposes of the qualification (*Abel* v. *Lee* (1871), L. R. 6 C. P. 365); and a purely voluntary payment by a stranger is not sufficient. (*Reg.* v. *The Mayor of Bridgnorth* (1839), 10 Ad. & Ell. 66.)

Parochial relief.

Parochial relief so as to disqualify does not include vaccination, or the surgical or medical assistance incident to vaccination performed or rendered by a public vaccinator (Vaccination Act, 1867, 30 & 31 Vict. c. 84, s. 26); or the payment of school fees by the guardians for the child of any person not being a pauper (Elementary Education Act, 1876, 39 & 40 Vict. c. 79, s. 10); or the admission of any person suffering from an infectious disease into any hospital provided by the Metropolitan Asylum Managers (Diseases Prevention (Metropolis) Act, 1883, 46 & 47 Vict. c. 35, s. 7); or the receipt of medical relief at the expense of the parish (Medical Relief Disqualification Removal Act, 1885, 48 & 49 Vict. c. 46), and this has been held to include a payment made by the relieving officer, in accordance with a resolution of the guardians, in respect of the attendance of an uncertificated midwife upon the voter's wife. (*Honeybone* v. *Hambridge* (1886), 18 Q. B. D. 418.) But parochial relief so as to disqualify generally includes any payment made out of the parish funds for the relief of a voter, or those whom he is by law bound to support, even though there may be some consideration in return for it. For instance, it includes a payment for work done made out of the parish funds, but at more than the value of the work to the guardians. (*Magarill* v. *The Overseers of Whitehaven* (1887), 16 Q. B. D. 242.) Those whom a voter is by law bound to support are his wife, and his children under the age of sixteen (Poor Law Act, 4 & 5 Will. 4, c. 76, s. 56); but he is not bound to support his parents, except on an order of justices, and so relief to his parent does not disqualify a voter. (*Reg.* v. *Ireland* (1868), L. R. 3 Q. B. 130.)

Notes to Sect. 2. Excusal from payment of poor rate on the ground of poverty does not disqualify. (*Mashiter* v. *Dunn* (1848), 6 C. B. 30.) Other alms disqualify in any case where there are present the three elements of poverty, the receipt of alms, and the absence of that independence which is essential to the qualification of a voter, all of which must co-exist in the particular case. (*Harrison* v. *Carter* (1876), 2 C. P. D. 26.) For instance, if a local charity provides aged and infirm inhabitants, not being able to maintain themselves by their own exertions, with lodgings in almshouses and a weekly allowance, they would be disqualified thereby. (*Baker* v. *The Town Clerk of Monmouth* (1885), 34 W. R. 64; *Edwards* v. *Lloyd* (1887), 20 Q. B. D. 302.)

Occupation of part of house.

Section 31 of the Municipal Corporations Act, 1882 (45 & 46 Vict. c. 50), as applied by this sub-section, will read as follows, viz.:—

In and for the purposes of this Act,—

(*a*) The terms "house," "warehouse," "counting-house," "shop," "or other building," include any part of a house, where that part is separately occupied for the purposes of any trade, business, or profession; and any such part may, for the purpose of describing the qualification, be described as office, chambers, studio, or by any like term applicable to the case.

(*b*) Where an occupier is entitled to the sole and exclusive use of any part of a house, that part shall not be deemed to be occupied otherwise than separately, by reason only that the occupier is entitled to the joint use of some other part.

Apart from this enactment, part of a house, though called by itself a house in the common understanding of the word, does not become a house in law unless there is an actual structural severance of such part from the rest of the building (*Cook* v. *Humber* (1861), 11 C. B. (N.S.) 33); but it was held in *Aldridge's case* that from the wording of sub-section (*b*) above cited, the term "house," as used in the Municipal Corporations Act, 1882, includes any part of a house not structurally severed from the rest of a building, where such part is separately occupied for the purposes of residence (*Greenway* v. *Batchelor* (*Aldridge's case*) (1883), 12 Q. B. D. 381), the same point having been provided for in respect of the parliamentary franchise, by the fifth section of the Parliamentary and Municipal Registration Act, 1878 (41 & 42 Vict. c. 26).

Notes to Sect. 2.

Rules as to qualification of county electors on succession, &c.

Section 33 of the Municipal Corporations Act, 1882 (45 & 46 Vict. c. 50), as applied by this sub-section, will read as follows, viz.:—

(1) Where a person succeeds to qualifying property by descent, marriage, marriage settlement, devise, or promotion to a benefice or office, then, for the purposes of qualification, the occupancy of the property by a predecessor in title, and the rating of the predecessor in respect thereof, shall be equivalent to the occupancy and rating of the successor; and rating in the name of the predecessor shall, until a new rate is made after the date of succession, be equivalent to rating in the name of the successor; and the successor shall not be required to prove his own residence, occupancy, or rating before the succession.

(2) The qualifying property need not be throughout the twelve months constituting the period of qualification the same property, or in the same parish.

(3) Where by law a *county* rate is payable by instalments, payment by any person of any such instalment shall, as regards his qualification to be registered as a *county elector* be deemed a payment of the *county* rate in respect of the period to which the instalment applies.

(4) A person shall not be disentitled to be registered as a *county elector* by reason only—

(*a*) That he has received medical or surgical assistance from the trustees of the *county* charities, or has been removed by order of a justice to a hospital

Notes to Sect. 2.

or place for reception of the sick at the cost of any local authority; or

(*b*) That his child has been admitted to and taught in any public or endowed school.

Right of women to vote.

Section 63 of the Municipal Corporations Act, 1882 (45 & 46 Vict. c. 50), as applied by this sub-section will read as follows, viz.:—

For all purposes connected with and having reference to the right to vote at *county (local government) elections*, words in this Act importing the masculine gender include women.

This section, as applied, does not entitle a married woman to be registered as a county elector, although she may be living separately from her husband and, but for the fact of the marriage, may be otherwise duly qualified by occupation and rating to be registered as a county elector, because a married woman is not in law "a person" within the meaning of the ninth section as applied, her legal existence being merged on the marriage in that of her husband so long as he continues alive and the marriage is not dissolved by the decree of a competent court. (*Reg.* v. *Harrald* (1872), L. R. 7 Q. B. 361.)

"Enactments of that or any other Act affecting the same." Probably this refers, amongst other sections which will be noted hereinafter, to section 32 of that Act and to the Municipal Voters Relief Act, 1885 (48 Vict. c. 9).

Claim to be rated and tender of rates.

Section 32 of the Municipal Corporations Act, 1882 (45 & 46 Vict. c. 50), as applied by this sub-section, will read as follows, viz.:—

(1) If an occupier of any qualifying property, whether the landlord is or is not liable to be rated in the poor rate in respect thereof, claims to be rated to the poor rate in respect thereof, and pays or tenders to the overseers of the parish where the property is situate the full amount of the poor rate last made in respect of the property, the overseers shall put the occupier's name on the rate book in respect of that rate.

Notes to Sect. 2.

A claim and tender need only be made if the overseers have altogether refused to rate any person whatever in respect of the premises to rates made during the required period of occupation, but it is not equivalent to rating and payment unless it is made during the required period of occupation. (*Ainsworth* v. *Creeke* (1868), L. R. 4 C. P. 476.) There is probably no necessity to repeat the claim and tender every time a fresh rate is made during the required period of occupation, but it may be made once for all so long as the voter remains in occupation of the same premises during that period. (14 & 15 Vict. c. 14.)

Letting furnished house.

Section 2 of the Municipal Voters Relief Act, 1885 (48 Vict. c. 9), as applied by this sub-section, will read as follows, viz.:—

> A man shall not be disqualified from being registered or voting as a *county elector* at any *county (local government) election* in a *county* in respect of the occupation of any house by reason only that during a part of the qualifying period, not exceeding four months in the whole, he has, by letting or otherwise, permitted such house to be occupied as a furnished dwelling-house by some other person, and during such occupation by another person has not resided in or within seven miles of the *county*.

The limit of four months must not be exceeded, or the occupier will be disqualified. As, for instance, undergraduates of the Universities of Oxford and Cambridge, who are not allowed to occupy their chambers in college during the vacations, which extend over a period of six months, are thereby disqualified. (*Tanner* v. *Carter* (1885), 16 Q. B. D. 231.)

Occupation of land of the value of 10*l.* to qualify.

3. Every person who is entitled to be registered as a voter in respect of a ten pounds occupation qualification within the meaning of the provisions of the Registration Act, 1885, which are set out in the schedule to this Act, shall be

Sect. 3. entitled to be registered as a county elector, and to be enrolled as a burgess, in respect of such qualification, in like manner in all respects as if the sections of the Municipal Corporations Act, 1882, relating to a burgess qualification included the said ten pounds occupation qualification.

Effect of section. The practical effect of this section will be to qualify every parliamentary ten pounds occupier in a parliamentary borough as a burgess or county elector, as the case may be.

But in a parliamentary county it will not be safe to take the list of parliamentary ten pounds occupiers as a list of persons qualified to be county electors or burgesses, as the case may be; first, because the payment of assessed taxes is no part of the parliamentary ten pounds occupation qualification in a parliamentary county, except within the area of a merged parliamentary borough; and, secondly, because in a parliamentary county, including the area of any merged parliamentary borough therein, there is a difference in the qualification of joint occupiers.

Generally with regard to this section, it is to be observed—

Subject-matter of qualification. That it makes land only, without any building upon it, a proper subject-matter of qualification.

That a "tenement" within the meaning of the section must be rateable, or such as but for being Crown property would be rateable, and must be capable of actual occupation. Incorporeal hereditaments, though sometimes rateable, as, for instance, sporting rights, are not considered capable of actual occupation for the purposes of an electoral qualification (*Druitt* v. *The Overseers of Christ Church* (1883), 12 Q. B. D. 365), so that a tenement practically means a building, and the occupier will be more likely to qualify under section 2, and not under this section.

Value. The principles upon which the clear yearly value is to be ascertained are well known in respect of the parliamen-

Notes to Sect. 3.

tary ten pounds occupation qualification, and apply equally for the purposes of the local government franchise under this section. They are discussed at length in "Mackenzie and Lushington on Parliamentary and Local Government Registration."

Estate.

In the same work will be found full consideration of the words "as owner or tenant," which import that the person in physical occupation must have either an estate, in the legal sense of the term, in the land,or else must be a lessee for a term. Occupation by mere permission, or as a guest, servant, lodger, or member of a corporate body will not qualify.

Residence.

It will be noticed that the required period of residence for the purposes of a ten pounds occupation qualification under this section is only six months immediataly preceding the 15th July in the year of registration, as against twelve months, which is the required period for the purposes of a general occupation qualification under section 2.

What constitutes residence has been already noted under section 2, and the whole subject will be found fully discussed in "Mackenzie and Lushington on Registration," Chapter II., section 2, in treating of the parliamentary ten pounds occupation qualification.

Rating and payment of rates and taxes.

The principal points as to rating and payment of rates have been noted under section 2. It may be observed here that payment of county rate is no part of this ten pounds occupation qualification, as it is in the case of a general occupation qualification under section 2. But payment of assessed taxes, which is no part of the general occupation qualification under section 2, is necessary for a ten pounds occupation qualification. Assessed taxes are such taxes as vary in amount in proportion to the value of the property in respect of which they are imposed, as the property tax, the house tax, and the land tax. By the fourth section of the Property Tax Act, 1842 (5 & 6 Vict. c. 35), non-payment of property tax will not disqualify, so that inhabited house duty alone remains to be considered. This tax becomes payable, without any demand made upon the occupier, on or before the 1st of January in every year. (Customs and

Notes to Sect. 3. Inland Revenue Duties Act, 1869, 32 & 33 Vict. c. 14, s. 8.) By the twelfth section of the Parliamentary Registration Act, 1843 (6 & 7 Vict. c. 18), the collectors of taxes must, within two days after the 20th July, send in to the overseers a list of defaulters in payment of assessed taxes, which it is the duty of the overseers to keep open for inspection for a fortnight after publication of the lists of occupation voters.

Joint occupiers.

Joint occupiers will be entitled to be registered as county electors or as burgesses, if the value of the land or tenement is such as to give ten pounds or more for each occupier, although in a parliamentary county, including the area of any merged borough therein, two only of such occupiers are entitled to be registered as parliamentary voters, unles they derived the property by descent, succession, marriage, marriage settlement, or devise, or unless they are *bonâ fide* engaged as partners carrying on trade or business thereon, in any of which cases all may be registered, if the value is sufficient to give ten pounds for each occupier. (Representation of the People Act, 1867, 30 & 31 Vict. c. 102, s. 27.)

Rights of women and peers.

Even in a parliamentary borough the list of parliamentary ten pounds occupiers will not be necessarily an exhaustive list of the persons qualified as burgesses or county electors under this section, for women and peers may be qualified as ten pounds burgesses or county electors, though not as parliamentary ten pounds occupiers. There will, however, be the same limitation on the right of women to vote as that which has been already pointed out in respect of the general occupation qualification under section 2, viz., that during coverture they have no legal personality apart from their husbands.

Registration of county electors.

41 & 42 Vict. c. 26.

4.—(1.) The Registration of Electors Acts shall, so far as circumstances admit, apply to the enrolment of burgesses in a municipal borough to which the Parliamentary and Municipal Registration Act, 1878, does not apply, and to the registration of county electors within the meaning of this Act; and the lists of burgesses, and of county electors, and of occupation voters for parliamentary elections, shall, so far as practicable, be made out and revised together; and the Registration of Electors Acts shall accordingly— Sect. 4.

(*a*) apply to every such municipal borough in like manner as if it were a borough to which sub-section two of section six of the Registration Act, 1885, applied (sub-section one of which section is hereby repealed), and revising assessors for such borough shall not be elected; and

(*b*) apply to every parish not situate in a municipal borough, in like manner as if such parish were a municipal borough to which the Parliamentary and Municipal Registration Act, 1878, applies, and the said lists of county electors and of occupation voters for parliamentary elections in such parish shall be made out in divisions, as provided in the said Act: Provided that a person whose name appears in any list of county electors or burgesses in a county may object to the name of any other person on a list of county electors or burgesses for a parish in that county, and may oppose the

Sect. 4.

claim of a person to have his name inscribed in any such list.

(2.) In the construction of the Registration of Electors Acts for the purpose of their application to a parish not situate in a municipal borough, there shall be made the variations following, and such other variations as may be necessary for carrying into effect the application, that is to say:—

(*a*) Where such parish is not within a parliamentary borough, "parliamentary county" shall be substituted for "parliamentary borough:"

(*b*) Where such parish is not within a parliamentary borough, the clerk of the peace shall perform the duties of and be substituted for the town clerk; but any notice required to be given to the town clerk by section twenty-seven of the Parliamentary and Municipal Registration Act, 1878, relating to the withdrawal and revival of objections, shall be given to the overseers and not to the clerk of the peace;

(*c*) County elector shall be substituted for burgess;

(*d*) Section nine of the Parliamentary and Municipal Registration Act, 1878, shall not apply to any parish which is not wholly situate in an urban district; Sect. 4.

(*e*) Where such parish is not within a parliamentary borough, section twenty-one of the Parliamentary and Municipal Registration Act, 1878, shall not apply, and the lists and register of voters shall be made out alphabetically, but shall be framed in parts for polling districts and electoral divisions and for urban districts and for wards of urban and rural districts in such a manner that the parts may be conveniently compiled or put together to serve as lists for polling districts, and elections in urban districts and as electoral division or ward lists;

(*f*) Where such parish is within a parliamentary borough—

(i.) the overseers shall send to the clerk of the peace for the county two copies of the lists of voters at the same time at which they send copies to the town clerk; and

(ii.) the town clerk shall cause to be printed such number of copies of the revised lists as the clerk of the peace may require, and shall transmit the same to the clerk of the peace, who shall

Sect. 4.

deal with the same as with other lists of county electors in his county; but,

(iii.) save as aforesaid, the clerk of the peace shall not act in relation to the registration of county electors in the said parish, and the town clerk of the parliamentary borough shall be the town clerk within the meaning of the Registration of Electors Acts and this Act in relation to such parish, and shall include in his precept to the overseers proper directions respecting the registration of the county electors within the meaning of this Act.

(*g*) The lists of occupation voters and county electors shall be revised by the revising barrister for the parliamentary borough or county in which such parish is situate, and the revising barrister for revising the county electors' lists for the whole or any part of an electoral division of any county shall, if so required by the county council, hold a court in that electoral division or at some convenient place in a division adjoining thereto.

(*h*) The guardians of a union which is not wholly comprised in an urban district may, with the consent of the overseers

Sect. 4.

of any parish or parishes within their union for which an assistant overseer has not been appointed, annually appoint a fit person to act as registration officer for such parish or parishes, and may remove any such person, and fill up any vacancy caused by death, resignation, or otherwise. Such registration officer shall perform all the duties of overseers of the parish or parishes for which he is appointed in respect of the registration of county electors and parliamentary voters, and the provisions of the Registration of Electors Acts relating to overseers, including those providing for penalties, shall apply to him accordingly:

Provided that his remuneration shall be fixed and paid by the guardians of the union, and charged on the poor rates of the parish or parishes for which he is appointed, and (if he acts for more than one parish) in proportion to the number of persons on the registers made during the year of his appointment of county electors and parliamentary voters for each parish.

(3.) Notwithstanding anything in this Act contained, where a municipal borough or an urban

Sect. 4. district is co-extensive with any electoral division or divisions of a parliamentary county, the lists of voters may be directed by the county authority to be made out according to the order in which the qualifying premises appear in the rate book, and section twenty-one of the Parliamentary and Municipal Registration Act, 1878, shall apply to such borough or urban district, and where lists of voters are so made out nothing in this Act shall require such part of the county register as consists of these lists to be arranged alphabetically.

Sub-sect. 1. Boroughs to which the Act of 1878 applies.

The Parliamentary and Municipal Registration Act, 1878 (41 & 42 Vict. c. 26), applies to any municipal borough wholly or partly comprised within the area of an existing parliamentary borough, or of a former parliamentary borough which ceased after the dissolution of the Parliament existing in January, 1885, to be a parliamentary borough. A list of these former parliamentary boroughs is contained in the first schedule to the Redistribution of Seats Act, 1885 (48 & 49 Vict. c. 23).

Application of s. 6 (2) of the Act of 1885.

Sub-section two of section six of the Registration Act, 1885 (48 Vict. c. 15), enacts that where any part of the area of a municipal borough was immediately before the dissolution of the then existing Parliament included in the area of a parliamentary borough, and such parliamentary borough ceased after such dissolution to be a parliamentary borough, then the registration of (parliamentary) occupation voters and the enrolment of burgesses in a parish in such municipal borough shall be conducted in like manner, so nearly as may be, as heretofore, and the Parliamentary and Municipal Registration Act, 1878, shall apply to the said municipal borough in like manner as heretofore, subject, nevertheless, as follows :

Notes to Sect. 4.

(*a*) "Parliamentary county" shall, for the purpose of such application, be substituted for "parliamentary borough."

(*b*) The lists and register of voters shall be made out alphabetically in like manner as in the rest of the county, but the lists shall be framed in parts for polling districts and wards in such manner that the parts may be conveniently compiled or put together to serve as lists for polling districts or as ward lists.

(*c*) The overseers of every parish in such municipal borough shall send to the clerk of the peace for the parliamentary county two copies of the lists of voters at the same time at which they send copies to the town clerk, and the lists of voters for a parish in such borough when revised shall be transmitted by the revising barrister to such clerk of the peace, and dealt with by him as with other lists in his county, but, save as aforesaid, the town clerk of the municipal borough shall, until such transmission, act as and be deemed to be the town clerk within the meaning of the Parliamentary Registration Acts and this Act in relation to such parish, and the clerk of the peace shall not act in relation to the registration of (parliamentary) occupation voters in such parish.

(*d*) The lists of (parliamentary) occupation voters and burgesses shall be revised by the revising barrister for the parliamentary county in which the municipal borough is situate, and if that borough extends into more parliamentary counties than one, then by the revising barrister for the parliamentary county in which the greater part in extent of such municipal borough is situate, and such revising barrister shall hold a court in the municipal borough.

Effect of application

The immediate practical effect of the application of this sub-section of the Registration Act, 1885, will be to render

Notes to Sect. 4. of the Act of 1885.

it necessary for the town clerk of such a municipal borough to issue a supplemental precept to the overseers of parishes within, or partly within, the borough relating to the enrolment of burgesses in this present year. In future years the town clerk will issue a precept for the registration both of the parliamentary occupation voters and of the burgesses to the overseers in such municipal boroughs, and the clerk of the peace will confine his precept to parliamentary ownership voters.

The overseers will have to perform the like duties in relation to the preparation and publication of lists of burgesses, notices as to payment of rates, and other documents, and other like duties as if the parish were situate in a parliamentary as well as in a municipal borough.

The lists will be revised by the revising barrister for the parliamentary county as provided for by the last paragraph of the applied sub-section, and not by the mayor and revising assessors under the Municipal Corporations Act, 1882 (45 & 46 Vict. c. 50), as formerly.

Abolition of revising assessors in non-parliamentary boroughs.

The revising assessors, who are abolished by this sub-section, were elected annually by the burgesses in every borough of which no part was included in the area of a parliamentary borough, or of a former parliamentary borough which ceased after the dissolution of the Parliament existing in January, 1885, to be a parliamentary borough, and their duties were to assist the mayor in the judicial business of revising the burgess lists.

The twenty-ninth section of the Municipal Corporations Act, 1882 (45 & 46 Vict. c. 50), relating to these revising assessors, is therefore impliedly repealed by this sub-section.

Lists made out in divisions.

The application of the Registration of Electors Acts to a parish not situate in a municipal borough is considerably modified by sub-section (2), which will be presently discussed, but it may be noted here that the making out of the occupiers' list "in divisions, as provided by the said Act" (*i.e.*, the Act of 1878), refers to section 15 of that Act, whereby the said list is to be made out in three divisions, and, as applied,—

Division One will comprise the names of the persons entitled to be registered both as parliamentary occupation voters other than lodgers and as county electors; **Notes to Sect. 4.**

Division Two will comprise the names of the persons entitled to be registered as parliamentary occupation voters other than lodgers, but not as county electors; and

Division Three will comprise the names of persons entitled to be registered as county electors, but not as parliamentary occupation voters.

The effect of this will be that Division Two will contain the names of service occupiers, and probably of some fifty pounds occupiers who may not be qualified as county electors in respect of the same property, and possibly of some ten pounds occupiers of property for which the assessed taxes have not been paid, and who have not resided for the whole year so as to qualify as burgess occupiers. Division Three will contain the names of women and peers who are occupiers of property qualifying for the local government franchise, and the names of the third and others of joint ten pounds occupiers where more than two persons are joint occupiers of property of sufficient value, but not coming within the exceptions in section 27 of the Representation of the People Act, 1867 (30 & 31 Vict. c. 102).

Supplemental lists.

In the present year, where a parish is not within a municipal borough, nor situated in a parliamentary borough, the clerk of the peace may, under section 15 of this Act, instead of directing the overseers to make out the occupiers' lists in divisions, direct them to make out supplemental lists containing the names which would otherwise be contained in Divisions Two and Three respectively. The person acting as town clerk of a parliamentary borough has no express power to direct the overseers of a parish in a parliamentary, but not in a municipal borough to follow that course, and must apparently direct the overseers to make out the occupiers' list in divisions.

Objections.

The person objected to will have a right to see whether the conditions imposed by the Registration of Electors

Notes to Sect. 4. Acts have been fulfilled, and, if they have not, to take advantage of that fact to defeat the objection. The overseers, therefore, will have no right to waive the delivery to them in due time of a valid notice of objection. (See per COLERIDGE, C.J., in *Freeman* v. *Newman* (1883), 12 Q. B. D. 375.) It will not be necessary, however, that a separate notice of objection should be given to the overseers in respect of each person objected to, but a single notice with a schedule containing the names of all persons objected to, with their respective places of abode and qualifications as described in the list, will be sufficient, provided that the same grounds of objection apply equally to all. (*Smith* v. *Holloway* (1865), L. R. 1 C. P. 145.) The necessary contents of a notice of objection are fully discussed in "Mackenzie and Lushington on Registration," Chapter V.; but it may be noted here that the notice should properly specify the list and division of the list to which the objection refers, and should be properly dated and signed by the objector, and under his signature the objector should state his true place of abode, so as to afford a full and sufficient address if a letter is addressed to him by post. The notice should also specify the list on which the objector's name appears, being a list which under this Act gives him the right to object. In specifying the list and division to which the objection refers, the "division" means either Division One or Division Three of the Occupiers' List, as noted in the earlier part of the notes to this sub-section (see per COLERIDGE, C.J., *Hall* v. *Cropper* (1879), 5 C. P. D. 81); and where that list is not made out in divisions, but supplemental lists are made out under the transitory provisions for 1888 under section fifteen of this Act, the notice must specify whether the objection refers to the general list or to the supplemental list corresponding to Division Three.

Claims. The overseers must not put the name of any person in the list of claimants as county electors or burgesses unless such person has sent them a proper notice of claim in due time, and the revising barrister will not be bound to allow any such claim unless he is satisfied that due notice was given to the overseers. (*In re Sale* (1880), 50 L. J. C. P. 113.)

Notes to Sect. 4.

Sub-sect. 2.

This sub-section, which relates to the construction of the Registration of Electors Acts for the purpose of their application to a parish not situate in a municipal borough, consists of three separate portions, the first comprising paragraphs (*a*) to (*e*) inclusive, and relating to such a parish when it is not within a parliamentary borough, the second comprising paragraphs (*e*) to (*g*) inclusive, and relating to such a parish when it is within a parliamentary borough, and the last consisting of paragraph (*h*), a novel and remarkable enactment.

Withdrawal and revival of objections.

As to the first group of paragraphs, in paragraph (*b*), section twenty-seven of the Parliamentary and Municipal Registration Act, 1878 (41 & 42 Vict. c. 26), relating to the withdrawal and revival of objections (as applied by this sub-section), provides that an objection may be withdrawn by a notice to that effect in writing, signed by the objector, and given to the person objected to, and to the overseers, not less than seven days before the day which shall be appointed for the holding of the first court of revision of the list to which the objection relates, and any objection by a qualified objector may, after his death, be revived by any other person qualified to have made the objection originally by a notice to that effect in writing, signed by him, and given to the person objected to, and to the overseers at or before the time of the revision of the entry to which the objection relates, and a person reviving an objection shall be deemed to have made the objection originally, and he shall be responsible in respect thereof, and the proceedings thereon shall be continued accordingly. Where an objection is made otherwise than by an overseer to any person whose name appears on a list of voters and county electors, and the name is retained on the list, the revising barrister shall, unless he is of opinion that the objection was reasonably made either because of a defect or error in the entry to which the objection relates, or because of a difficulty in verifying or identifying the particulars comprised in such entry, or unless the objection is duly with-

Notes to Sect. 4.

drawn, or unless for some other special reason he otherwise determines, order costs, not exceeding forty shillings, to be paid by the objector to the person objected to.

But, generally, if any correction is made, although the name is retained the barrister will not make an order for costs, because the alteration generally shows good cause for objecting.

In paragraph (*d*) of this sub-section, section nine of the Parliamentary and Municipal Registration Act, 1878, therein referred to, relates to the publication of lists and notices in postal and telegraph offices. In paragraph (*e*), section twenty-one of the same Act therein referred to relates to the arrangement of the lists and registers according to streets.

Polling districts.

Polling districts for the first election of county councillors are to be settled by the sheriff, as returning officer, or the person appointed as returning officer in case the sheriff is a candidate (L. G. B. sect. 99), so that the overseers will not be troubled with framing the lists of county electors in the present year with reference to polling districts.

Electoral divisions.

Electoral divisions in boroughs returning more than one county councillor are to be determined by the council of the borough, but any borough returning one county councillor only is to be an electoral division of itself, and in the rest of the county the quarter sessions are to determine the electoral divisions. The Local Government Board will, in the first place, determine the number of elective councillors, and their apportionment between each of the boroughs which have sufficient population to return one councillor and the rest of the county. (L. G. B. sect. 3.)

Urban and rural districts are by section fourteen of this Act defined to mean respectively an urban or rural sanitary district, also any urban or rural district under the Local Government Bill when it has passed into law.

Town clerks.

As to the second group of paragraphs relating to a parish not within a municipal, but within a parliamentary borough, it may be useful to remember that where a municipal borough forms part of a parliamentary borough the town clerk of the municipal borough is the town clerk of the parliamentary borough within the meaning of the Registration of Electors Acts. (Parliamentary Electors Registration Act, 1868, 31 & 32 Vict. c. 58, s. 18.) In other parliamentary boroughs the returning officer acts as town clerk (Parliamentary Registration Act, 1843, 6 & 7 Vict. c. 18, s. 101), but in the city of London the expression town clerk means the secondaries, and in the city of Westminster the bailiff, and in the borough of Southwark the high bailiff. (Parliamentary Registration Act, 1843, 6 & 7 Vict. c. 18, s. 56.)

Notes to Sect. 4.

Registration officer.

The last paragraph of this sub-section may possibly not be taken advantage of in this present year, considering the lateness of the passing of this Act with regard to the dates fixed for carrying its provisions into effect, and possibly by next year the Government may have in hand their promised scheme dealing generally with the subject of registration, in which it is very likely that new registration officers will be created to take over the duties of overseers generally.

Assistant overseers.

Assistant overseers are "overseers" within the meaning of the Registration of Electors Acts (see Parliamentary Registration Act, 1843, 6 & 7 Vict. c. 18, s. 101), and are appointed under section seven of Sturgis Bourne's Act (59 Geo. 3, c. 12) by warrant of two justices on the nomination of the vestry to do such duties for such salary as the vestry may specify, and they hold office until resignation or the revocation of their appointment by the vestry.

Rate books.

This paragraph makes no express provision that the registration officer, if appointed, should have access to the rate books, and it will be absolutely necessary that he should have access to them if he is to do his work properly. But as he cannot be appointed without the consent of the overseers, it is not likely that any difficulty will arise between them about it. The registration officer will have to produce the rate books, containing rates made during the past two years, at the revision court.

Sub-sect. 3. Lists to be made out according to streets.

Section twenty-one of the Parliamentary and Municipal Registration Act, 1878 (41 & 42 Vict. c. 26), herein referred to, as applied, provides that if and so far as the county

Notes to Sect. 4.

authority so direct, the lists of parliamentary voters, and register of parliamentary voters, and the burgess and county electors' lists, and burgess rolls, and the county register, and the lists of claimants and persons objected to, or any of those documents, in any municipal borough or urban district co-extensive with any electoral division or divisions of a county, shall, so far as they relate to persons qualified in respect of the ownership or occupation of property (including persons qualified in respect of lodgings), be arranged in the same order in which the qualifying premises appear in the rate book for the parish in which those premises are situate, or as nearly thereto as will cause those lists, registers, and rolls to record the qualifying premises in successive order in the street or other place in which they are situate, subject in the case of a municipal borough divided into wards to the division of the burgess roll into ward lists, and subject in the case of a municipal borough or urban district co-extensive with more electoral divisions than one to the division of the county register into division registers.

Under section fifty-one of the Local Government Bill an electoral division is not to consist of portions of two or more county districts, but a county district may be divided into two or more electoral divisions.

Making out of lists and registers in the metropolis.

5. After the year one thousand eight hundred and eighty-eight, in every part of the metropolis, and in every part of a parliamentary borough, the whole or greater part of which is situate in the metropolis, the lists and registers of parliamentary voters, and of county electors, shall, unless the local authority otherwise direct, be arranged in the same order in which the qualifying premises appear in the rate book for the parish in which those premises are situate, or as nearly thereto as will cause those lists and registers to record the qualifying premises in successive order in the street or other place in which they are situate. Sect. 5.

For the purpose of this section "metropolis" means the city of London and the parishes and places mentioned in Schedules (A.), (B.), and (C.) of the Metropolis Management Act, 1855. 18 & 19 Vict. c. 120.

Arrangement of metropolitan list of voters.

This section is practically an application of the twenty-seventh section of the Parliamentary and Municipal Registration Act, 1878 (41 & 42 Vict. c. 26), extended (so as to include county electors' lists) to the Metropolis, unless the local authority otherwise direct, instead of if they so direct. The local authority seems to mean in every parliamentary borough, wholly or partly included in that area, the authority having power to divide such borough into polling districts, and as regards a municipal borough, the council, and as regards the city of London, the Court of Aldermen.

The Metropolis as defined in this section is the new county of London proposed to be created under the Local Government Bill.

Revision of electoral lists.

6.—(1.) The lists of parliamentary voters, and of burgesses, and of county electors, shall be revised between the eighth day of September and the twelfth day of October both inclusive, and shall be revised as soon as possible after the seventh day of September, and the eighth day of September shall be substituted in the Acts relating to the registration of parliamentary voters for the fifteenth day of September; and the declarations under section ten of the County Voters Regis- 28 & 29 Vict. c. 36.

Sect. 6. tration Act, 1865, and section twenty-four of the Parliamentary and Municipal Registration Act, 1878, shall be sent to the clerk of the peace or town clerk on or before the fifth day of September.

41 & 42 Vict. c. 26.

(2.) In sections sixty-two and sixty-three of the Parliamentary Voters Registration Act, 1843 (relating to appeals from revising barristers in England), "the Michaelmas sittings of the High Court of Justice" shall be substituted for "the Michaelmas term," and forthwith after the fourth day of the Michaelmas sittings a court or courts shall sit for the purpose of hearing such appeals, and those appeals shall be heard and determined continuously and without delay, and any statement by the barrister for the purpose of any such appeal made in pursuance of section forty-two of the said Act may be made at any time within ten days after the conclusion of the revision, so that it be made not less than four days before the first day of the said Michaelmas sittings, and the statement need not be read in open court, but shall be submitted to the appellant, who, if he approves the same, shall sign the same as directed by the said section, and return the same to the barrister.

6 & 7 Vict. c. 18.

Sub-sect. 1. Dates for holding revision courts.

This sub-section alters the dates fixed for the holding of revision courts under the Parliamentary Registration Acts, and these courts will have in future to be held between the 8th September and 12th October, both inclusive, as provided

Notes to Sect. 6.

by this sub-section, whereas formerly they might be held in counties between the 15th September and 20th October (Parliamentary Registration Act, 1843, 6 & 7 Vict. c. 18, s. 32; County Voters Registration Act, 28 Vict. c. 36, s. 12), and in boroughs between the 15th September and the 31st October (Parliamentary Registration Act, 1843, 6 & 7 Vict. c. 18, s. 33), the last day for revising a burgess list being the 12th October (Parliamentary and Municipal Registration Act, 1878, 41 & 42 Vict. c. 26, s. 18).

But under section fifteen of this Act, in the year 1888 the time for revising the lists of county electors is extended to the 31st October.

Dates for declarations

The declarations under section ten of the County Voters Registration Act, 1865 (28 & 29 Vict. c. 36), in this sub-section referred to, are declarations by county voters, relating to change of abode, or objections founded on the second column of the list, which have to be transmitted to the clerk of the peace; and the declarations under section twenty-four of the Parliamentary and Municipal Registration Act, 1878 (41 & 42 Vict. c. 26), are declarations by borough voters as to misdescription, which have to be transmitted to the town clerk.

If a declaration is not sent to the clerk of the peace or town clerk, as the case may be, in due time, the revising barrister will have no power to accept it as evidence of the facts declared to, although the declaration may have been sent to the clerk of the peace or town clerk in time for the holding of the revision court. (*Daking* v. *Fraser* (1885), 16 Q. B. D. 252.)

Sub-sect. 2. Hearing of registration appeals.

The Michaelmas sittings of the High Court of Justice commence on the 24th October (Order in Council of the 12th December, 1883), so that the court for hearing the appeals from the revising barristers will commence to sit on the 28th of October. The court for hearing these appeals is a Divisional Court of the Queen's Bench Division. (Rules of the Supreme Court, O. 59, r. 1 (2).)

The provision that the case on appeal may be stated at any time within ten days after the conclusion of the revision so that it be made not less than four days before the first

Notes to Sect. 6.

day of the Michaelmas sittings, and that it need not be read in open court, disposes of the strict construction of section forty-two of the Parliamentary Voters Registration Act, 1843 (6 & 7 Vict. c. 18), which was so strongly entertained by the present Master of the Rolls in *Sherwin* v. *Whyman* (*Sherwin* v. *Whyman* (1873), L. R. 9 C. P. 247), and by others, and is more in accordance with the views of the Irish Court of Appeal upon the corresponding Irish statutes in *Topham* v. *Kelleher* (*Topham* v. *Kelleher* (1879), L. R. (Ireland) 6 C. L. 285); and by implication it must be taken, so it seems, to dispense with the necessity for the revising barrister signing the case and indorsement in open court before the conclusion of the revision as required by the same section.

Dates for appeals in the year 1888.

The dates fixed by this sub-section, when considered with reference to the transitory provisions for the present year contained in section fifteen of this Act, do not appear to have been well arranged.

Under section fifteen, the time for the completion of the revision for the present year is extended to the thirty-first of October, but the court of appeal from the revising barristers must under this sub-section now under discussion commence to sit on the twenty-eighth of October. Then, by section sixty-two of the Parliamentary Voters Registration Act, 1843 (6 & 7 Vict. 18), as altered by the Judicature Acts and by this sub-section now under discussion, it is absolutely necessary to enter in the Central Office notice of intention to prosecute the appeal within the first four days of the Michaelmas sittings, that is to say, from the twenty-fourth to the twenty-seventh of October inclusive, and it has been decided that unless this notice is entered in due time the court has no jurisdiction to entertain the appeal (*Autey* v. *Topham* (1843), 5 M. & G. 1; *Simpson* v. *Wilkinson*, *ibid.* 3*n*). Again, under section sixty-four of the Parliamentary Voters Registration Act, 1843 (6 & 7 Vict. c. 18), the appellant must give to the respondent a notice in writing of his intention to prosecute the appeal at least ten days before the first day appointed for the hearing of the appeals, and if this has not been done the court have no power to adjourn the hearing where ten clear days have elapsed between the date of the decision of the revising barrister and the first day fixed for hearing the appeals (*Luckett* v. *Gilder* (1861), 11 C. B. (N.S.) 1), although under the proviso to section sixty-four the court may adjourn the hearing if there were not ten clear days between the date of the decision of the revising barrister and the first day fixed for the hearing of the appeals. **Notes to Sect. 6.**

All right of appeal, therefore, will be lost in cases where the revising barrister postpones his decision after the 27th of October; and where he postpones it after the 17th of October, unless application is made to the court to adjourn the hearing so as to give time for ten days' notice to be served on the respondent, the court will not adjourn it, and the appeal will be dismissed for want of giving such notice. If, however, the revising barrister gives his decision before the 17th of October, ten days' notice of intention to prosecute an appeal must be served on the respondent on or before the 17th, or the appeal will be dismissed for want of notice, and the court will have no power to adjourn the hearing even though an application were made to them for that object.

Roll of county electors

7.—(1.) The clerk of the peace of every county shall make up a register of all persons registered as burgesses or county electors in the county, both for the county and for each electoral division into which the county is divided for the purpose of election of the county authority, and such number of copies as the clerk of the peace may require of the list of burgesses as revised shall be delivered by the town clerk to such clerk of the peace for the purpose of making up such register.

Sect. 7.

(2.) The Registration of Electors Acts, and sections forty-five, forty-eight, and seventy-one of the Municipal Corporations Act, 1882, shall apply, for the purposes of this section, with the substitution of clerk of the peace for town clerk, and of county register and division register for burgess roll and ward roll respectively, and of electoral division for ward, and of county fund for borough fund.

45 & 46 Vict. c. 50.

(3.) If district councils are established under any Act of the present session of Parliament, the clerk of every such council, not being the council of a borough, shall make up a register of all persons registered as county electors in his district, and where there are wards in a district, of all county electors in each ward, and he shall obtain from the clerk of the peace a sufficient number of copies of the lists of the county electors so registered as may be required for the purpose of making up such register and supplying the same to the public, and the above-mentioned Acts and sections shall apply for that purpose, with the substitution of "clerk of the district council" for "town clerk," and of "district register" for "burgess roll" respectively;

(4.) Provided that nothing in this section shall prevent a county elector from being registered in more than one division register.

(5.) Where in pursuance of section four of the Registration Act, 1885, the revising barrister has power to erase the name of any person as a parliamentary voter from division one of the occupiers' list, such barrister, in lieu of erasing the name, shall place an asterisk or other mark against the name, and, in printing such lists, the name shall be numbered consecutively with the other names, but an asterisk or other mark shall be printed against the name, and a person against whose name such asterisk or other mark is placed shall not be entitled to vote in respect of such entry at a parliamentary election, but shall have the same right of voting at an election of a county authority as he would have if no such mark were placed against his name.

Sect. 7.

48 & 49 Vict. c. 15.

(6.) If under any Act of the present session of Parliament establishing a council for a county any portion of another county is added to that county for the purpose of such election, such portion of the county register as relates to the electors having qualifying property in the said part so added shall be deemed to be part of the county register of the county for which such council is elected, and the clerk of the peace and other officers shall take such steps as may be necessary for giving effect to these enactments.

County and district registers.

This section imposes on the clerk of the peace for the county a new duty, viz., that of making up the county

Notes to Sect. 7. register after the revising barristers have finished the business of revision; and, after the present year, if the Local Government Bill passes, it will also impose on the clerks of the new district councils the duty of making up the district register.

Sub-sect. 1. Electoral divisions. The constitution of electoral divisions has been already noted under section four, sub-section two, of this Act.

County authority. The expression "county authority" is in the preamble stated to mean any representative body which may be established under any Act of the present session of Parliament for the purposes of local government in counties in England, *i.e.*, the county and district councils intended to be established under the Local Government Bill.

Sub-sect. 2. Section forty-five of the Municipal Corporations Act 1882 (45 & 46 Vict. c. 50), as applied by this sub-section, will read as follows, viz.:

County register.

(1) When the parish burgess lists have been revised and signed, the revising *barrister* shall deliver them to the clerk of the peace, and a printed copy thereof, examined by him and signed by him, shall be (together with the revised parish county electors' lists) the *county register* of the *county*.

(2) The *county register* shall be completed on or before the 20th October in each year (the 31st day of December is by section fifteen substituted for the 20th of October in the year 1888), and shall come into operation on the 1st of November in that year (the 1st day of January in the year 1889 is by section fifteen substituted for the 1st of November, 1888, but not so as to continue the operation of that register beyond twelve months from the 1st November, 1888), and shall continue in operation for twelve months, beginning on that day.

(3) The names in the *county register* shall be numbered by *electoral divisions* or by polling districts, unless in any case the county council direct that the

same be numbered consecutively without reference to *electoral divisions* or polling districts.

(4) Where the *county* has no *electoral divisions*, the *county register* shall be made in one general register for the whole *county*.

Division registers

(5) Where the *county* has *electoral divisions*, the *county register* shall be made in separate registers, called *division registers*, one for each *electoral division*, containing the names of the persons entitled to vote in that *electoral division*, and the *division registers* collectively shall constitute the *county register*.

Duplicate lists.

(6) Where a duplicate of a parish burgess list is made under section thirty-one of the Parliamentary and Municipal Registration Act, 1878 (as applied by this Act), it shall have the same effect as the original, and may be delivered instead thereof.

(7) Every person *registered* in the *county register* shall be deemed to be enrolled as a burgess, and every person not registered in the county register shall be deemed to be not enrolled as a burgess.

(8) No stamp duty shall be payable in respect of the *registration* of any person in the *county register*.

Section thirty-one of the Parliamentary and Municipal Registration Act, 1878 (41 & 42 Vict. c. 26), as applied under this Act, and referred to in section forty-five of the Municipal Corporations Act, 1882 (45 & 46 Vict. c. 50), as applied under this sub-section, will read as follows, viz.:

Delivery of lists made in divisions under County Electors Act, 1888.

The lists, if made out in divisions under the County Electors Act, 1888, shall, when revised, be delivered to the clerk of the peace or town clerk, to whom, in respect of the area to which the lists relate, revised parliamentary lists ought to be delivered.

The revising barrister shall, as part of the business of the revision, at the request of the town clerk of any municipal borough the whole or part of the area of

Notes to Sect. 7.

which is included in the area of a parliamentary county, sign and deliver to him a duplicate of the whole or part of any revised list made out in divisions and relating to that municipal borough.

Every such duplicate shall be prepared by the town clerk at whose request it is so signed, and shall be kept by him for municipal purposes.

Section forty-eight of the Municipal Corporations Act, 1882 (45 & 46 Vict. c. 50), as applied by this sub-section, will read as follows, viz. :—

Printing and sale of county register.

(1) The *clerk of the peace* shall cause the *county electors' lists*, the lists of claimants and respondents (qy. persons objected to), and the *county register*, to be printed, and shall deliver printed copies to any person on payment of a reasonable price for each copy.

(2) Subject to section thirty of the Parliamentary and Municipal Registration Act, 1878 (and also subject to that section as applied by the County Electors Act, 1888), the proceeds of sale shall go to the *county fund*.

Section thirty of the Parliamentary and Municipal Registration Act, 1878 (41 & 42 Vict. c. 26), as applied by this Act, will read as follows, viz.:

Expenses and receipts where burgess lists are revised under the County Electors Act, 1888.

Where the whole or part of the area of a municipal borough is included in the area of a parliamentary county the expenses of the town clerk (including in his expenses the matters mentioned in section thirty-one of the Representation of the People Act, 1867 (30 & 31 Vict. 102), and the expenses properly incurred by the overseers in carrying into effect the provisions of the County Electors Act, 1888, with respect to the list of parliamentary voters and burgesses' lists, and all moneys received in respect of any of those lists, or in respect of any fine imposed by the revising barrister on the revision of the lists, shall respectively be paid and applied as follows:

(1) If the whole of the area of the municipal borough is included in the area of the parliamentary county, one half of the expenses shall be defrayed in the manner provided by the Parliamentary Registration Acts as expenses incurred thereunder, and the other half shall be defrayed out of the borough fund, and one half of the moneys received shall be applied in the manner directed in those Acts, and the other half shall be paid to the borough fund:

(2) In all other cases the expenses and receipts in respect of the area common to the parliamentary county and to the municipal borough be defrayed and applied as expenses and receipts under the Parliamentary Registration Acts, and shall, as to the other half thereof, be defrayed out of and paid to the borough fund of such municipal borough:

And the expenses and receipts of an area exclusively parliamentary shall be defrayed and applied as expenses and receipts under the Registration of Electors Acts, 1843 to 1888.

And the expenses and receipts in respect of an area exclusively municipal, shall be defrayed out of and paid to the borough fund of such municipal borough.

Any expenses and receipts incurred or arising in respect of more than one such area shall be apportioned between the several areas in respect of which they are incurred or arise, in the proportion as nearly as may be in which the same are incurred and arise in respect of the several areas, regard being had to the number of parliamentary voters or burgesses in each area, or any other circumstances occasioning the expense or giving rise to the receipts:

The revising barrister shall, as part of the business of the revision, determine, if necessary, in respect of

Notes to Sect. 7.

what area or areas any expenses or receipts are incurred or arise, and how much thereof is attributable to each area:

Section seventy-one of the Municipal Corporations Act, 1882 (45 and 46 Vict. c. 50), as applied by this sub-section, will read as follows, viz.:

Extended operation of county register.

(1) If a parish burgess list is not made or revised in due time, the corresponding part of the *county register* in operation before the time appointed for the revision shall be the parish burgess list until a burgess list for the parish has been revised and become part of the *county register*.

(2) If a *county register* is not made in due time, the *county register* in force before the time appointed for the revision shall continue in force until a new *county register* is made.

These provisions obviously cannot come into operation in the present year.

Sub-sect. 3. District register.

This sub-section does not apply to boroughs. District councils are dealt with in Part III. of the Local Government Bill, and the constitution of the district council in a county district, not being a borough, and the number of councillors and wards in such district are provided for by sections forty-three and forty-four of the bill. The duties of the clerk of such a council under this sub-section will be precisely similar to the duties now performed by the town clerk of a municipal borough in making up the burgess roll.

Sub-sect. 4. Registration in several divisions.

Under section forty-five of the Municipal Corporations Act, 1882 (45 & 46 Vict. c. 50), a burgess may not be enrolled in more than one ward roll, but under this subsection a county elector may be registered in more than one division register. There seems to be no reason why a person entered in the burgess roll for a municipal borough in a county may not be also entered as a county elector in more than one division register in the same county, provided that no such division register is for an electoral division including part of the same municipal borough.

This sub-section is necessary in order to give effect to the preceding sub-section, for, otherwise, where the name of a person appeared to be entered more than once in the lists of voters for the same parliamentary county, it would be the duty of the revising barrister, on proof that such entries related to the same person, to erase all such entries except one, which was to be selected to be retained as provided for by sub-section nine of section four of the Registration Act, 1885 (48 Vict. c. 15).

Notes to Sect. 7.
Sub-sect. 5.
Double entries.

The rules as to selection of the entry to be retained under that sub-section are—

(1) That the voter may select it by notice in writing to be delivered or sent by post to the revising barrister at or before the opening of the first court at which he revises any of the lists in which any such entries appear, or by application made by the voter or on his behalf at the time of the revision of the first of such lists:

(2) If no such selection is made, then if only one of the entries is on the list of ownership voters, that entry is to be retained; but if all or none of the entries are on the list of ownership voters, and one of the entries is the place of abode of the voter, the entry in respect of the place of abode is to be retained. In any other case the entry in that one of the lists which is first revised by the revising barrister must be retained.

Sub-sect. 6.
Alteration of boundaries.

This sub-section probably refers to future alterations of the boundaries of counties and boroughs under the fifty-seventh section of the Local Government Bill.

Expenses and receipts.

8.—(1.) All expenses properly incurred and all sums received in carrying into effect the provisions of this Act and the Registration of Electors Acts with respect to county electors,—

Sect. 8. (*a*) if incurred or received by overseers, shall be respectively paid and applied as expenses and receipts of overseers under the Registration of Electors Acts in the case of the lists of parliamentary voters; and

(*b*) if incurred or received by the clerk of the peace or town clerk, shall be paid out of or into the county or borough fund; and such expenses shall include all proper and reasonable fees and charges made and charged by him for the trouble, care, and attention of such clerk in the performance of the services and duties imposed on him by the said provisions.

Expenses and receipts of overseers. The expenses and receipts of overseers under the Registration of Electors Acts in the case of the lists of parliamentary voters are paid and applied as follows, viz.:—

By the fifty-seventh section of the Parliamentary Voters Registration Act, 1843 (6 & 7 Vict. c. 18), it is provided that an account of all expenses incurred by the overseers of every parish or township in carrying into effect the provisions of that Act shall be laid before the revising barrister at the court at which the list of voters for such parish or township shall be revised; and the said barrister shall sign and give to the said overseers a certificate of the sum which he shall allow to be due to them in respect of the said expenses; and it shall be lawful for the said overseers to receive the sum so certified to be due to them from and out of the first moneys thereafter to be collected for the relief of the poor in the same parish or township.

By the thirty-first section of the Parliamentary Electors Registration Act, 1868 (31 & 32 Vict. c. 58), all expenses properly incurred by an overseer in pursuance of that Act shall be deemed to be expenses properly incurred by him in carrying into effect the provisions of the principal Act (Parliamentary Voters Registration Act, 1843, 6 & 7 Vict. c. 18); and any expense incurred by any relieving officer in attending a revising barrister in pursuance of this Act (the amount to be certified by the revising barrister) shall be deemed to be expenses properly incurred by him in the execution of his duty as relieving officer, and shall be defrayed accordingly. **Notes to Sect. 8.**

And by the thirty-second section of the same Act, the certificate to be given to the overseers by the revising barrister under section fifty-seven of the principal Act for the expenses incurred by them in carrying into effect the provisions of the Registration Acts shall be final and conclusive; provided nevertheless, that such certificate shall be signed by the revising barrister in open court, and any ratepayer present shall have a right to inspect the account of expenses delivered in by the overseers, and to object to any item or items included therein, before such account is allowed by the revising barrister, who shall hear any such objection and make a decision respecting the same.

By the thirtieth section of the Parliamentary and Municipal Registration Act, 1878 (41 & 42 Vict. c. 26), where the whole or part of the area of a municipal borough is co-extensive with or included in the area of a parliamentary borough, the expenses properly incurred by the overseers in carrying into effect the provisions of this Act with respect to the lists of parliamentary voters and burgess lists, and all moneys received in respect of any of those lists, or in respect of any fine imposed by the revising barrister on the revision of the lists, shall be respectively paid and applied as follows:—

(1) If the area of the parliamentary borough and the area of the municipal borough are co-extensive, one-half of the expenses shall be defrayed in the manner provided by the Parliamentary Registration Acts as expenses incurred thereunder, and the

Notes to Sect. 8.

other half shall be defrayed out of the borough fund, and one-half of the moneys received as aforesaid shall be applied in the manner directed by those Acts, and the other half shall be paid to the borough fund :

(2) In all other cases, the expenses and receipts in respect of the area common to the parliamentary borough and to a municipal borough shall, as to one-half thereof, be defrayed and applied as expenses and receipts under the Parliamentary Registration Acts, and shall as to the other half thereof be defrayed out of and paid to the borough fund of such municipal borough :

And the expenses and receipts of an area exclusively parliamentary shall be defrayed and applied as expenses and receipts under the Parliamentary Registration Acts:

And the expenses and receipts of an area exclusively municipal shall be defrayed out of and paid to the borough fund of the municipal borough comprising such area:

Any expenses and receipts incurred or arising in respect of more than one such area shall be apportioned between the several areas in respect of which they are incurred or arise, in the proportion as nearly as may be in which the same are incurred and arise in respect of the several areas, regard being had to the number of parliamentary voters or burgesses in each area, or any other circumstances occasioning the expenses or giving rise to the receipts.

The revising barrister shall, as part of the business of the revision, determine, if necessary, in respect of what area or areas any expenses or receipts are incurred or arise, and how much thereof is attributable to each area.

Expenses and receipts of clerks of

As regards the payment and application of the expenses and receipts of the clerk of the peace and town clerk, the

Registration of Electors Acts provide in effect as follows, viz. :—

Notes to Sect. 8.

The peace and town clerks.

Their expenses were by section thirty-one of the Representation of the People Act, 1867 (30 & 31 Vict. c. 102), defined to include all proper and reasonable fees and charges for trouble, care, and attention in the performance of the services imposed by these Acts, and by section thirty-eight of the Parliamentary and Municipal Registration Act, 1878 (41 & 42 Vict. c. 26), to include also the expenses properly incurred by a clerk of the peace or town clerk as respondent to an appeal, including any costs which he might be ordered to pay to the appellant. The first of these enactments was passed in consequence of the decisions in *Reg.* v. *Kingston-upon-Hull* (1853), 2 Ell. & Bl. 182; *Reg.* v. *Kingston-upon-Hull* (1853), 25 L. T. 197; and *Reg.* v. *Allday* (1857), 26 L. J. Q. B. 292, to the effect that "expenses" under the Parliamentary Voters Registration Act, 1843 (6 & 7 Vict. c. 18), only included money actually paid or disbursed by the clerk of the peace or town clerk in respect of his services under that Act; and that is why the like enactment is contained in the paragraph now under discussion.

The receipts included the proceeds of sales of copies of the register, and the fines imposed by the revising barrister.

Of these expenses and receipts it was the duty of the clerk of the peace and town clerk respectively to keep accounts, and the clerk of the peace had to account for or pay over his receipts to the county treasurer, to be applied in aid of the county rate, and the town clerk had to account for or pay over his receipts to the overseers of the various parishes in his borough, to be applied in aid of the poor rate, each parish receiving a share proportionate to the number of its voters, as compared with the number on the lists for the other parishes in the same borough. (Parliamentary Voters Registration Act, 1843, 6 & 7 Vict. c. 18, s. 53.)

The account of the expenses of the clerk of the peace had to be laid before quarter sessions, and such expenses as

Notes to Sect. 8.

were allowed by quarter sessions were paid to him on their order out of the public stock of the county by the county treasurer. (*Ibid.* s. 54.)

The expenses of the town clerk were defrayed out of the poor rates, each parish contributing in proportion to the number of its voters as compared with the other parishes in the borough; and an account of the expenses, and of the contributions thereto payable by each parish, had to be laid before the town council, or before the quarter sessions, if the borough was only a parliamentary and not a municipal borough, and such amount as they allowed was paid by the overseers out of the poor rates accordingly. (*Ibid.* s. 56.)

The arrangement, however, which is made by the paragraph now under discussion assumes that the Local Government Bill will be passed in its present form, so far as the main outlines are concerned, before the payment and application of the expenses and receipts of this year's registration come to be settled, but by section eleven of this Act provision is made that in case that bill should not be passed in time, the expenses and receipts of the clerks of the peace and town clerks shall be paid and applied as formerly. If the bill does pass in time, the particular machinery for the payment of expenses, which is to supersede the present method of allowance and order, or certificate, will be provided for therein.

Remuneration of revising barristers and contribution by county authorities.

9. Every barrister appointed to revise any list of voters under the Parliamentary Voters Registration Act, 1843, shall be paid the sum of two hundred and fifty guineas by way of remuneration to him, and in satisfaction of his travelling and other expenses, and every such barrister, after the termination of his last sitting, shall forward his appointment to the Commissioners of Her Majesty's Treasury, who shall make an order for the payment of the above sum to every such barrister. **Notes to Sect. 9.**

The maximum amount to be paid to an additional barrister in pursuance of the Revising Barristers Act, 1886, shall not exceed the amount authorised by this section to be paid to a revising barrister. 49 & 50 Vict. c. 42.

The sums so paid to a revising barrister or an assistant barrister shall be payable partly out of moneys provided by Parliament and partly by the county authorities, as hereinafter mentioned.

(1.) There shall be annually paid by the county authority of every county out of the county fund into Her Majesty's Exchequer such sum as the Treasury certify to be one-half of the cost incurred for the payment of revising barristers at the then last revision of the lists of parliamentary electors, burgesses, and county electors in that county.

(2.) The Treasury shall yearly ascertain the total cost of the revising barristers appointed for all the counties and boroughs on any circuit, and shall divide one-half of such cost among the counties comprised in such circuit in proportion to the number of burgesses and county electors in each county, and certify the amount which under such apportionment is due under this section from each county. The Treasury may vary such certifi-

Sect. 9. cate if they think fit, but unless it is so varied the certificate shall be final.

(3.) So much of any Act as requires a payment out of the borough fund of any borough to a revising barrister, in respect of the revision of the burgess lists, shall be repealed, without prejudice to any payment or liability previously made or incurred.

Remuneration of revising barristers.

The salary of a revising barrister was fixed by the fifty-ninth section of the Parliamentary Registration Act, 1843 (6 & 7 Vict. c. 18, which is repealed by section ten of this Act), at the sum of 200 guineas, by way of remuneration to him and in satisfaction of his travelling and other expenses; and by the thirtieth section of the Parliamentary and Municipal Registration Act, 1878 (41 & 42 Vict. c. 26), and the third section of the Municipal Corporations Act, 1859 (22 Vict. c. 35, s. 3), which are the enactments repealed by sub-section three of this section, in the case of a municipal borough of which the burgess lists were revised together with the lists of parliamentary voters, the revising barrister was entitled to be paid out of the borough fund, by way of additional remuneration in respect of his additional work on account of the municipal revision for such municipal borough, a sum of five guineas a day over and above his travelling and other expenses.

In case of the death, illness, or absence of any revising barrister, the substitute appointed in his place is, under the first section of the Revising Barristers Act, 1874 (37 & 38 Vict. c. 18), to be paid out of the sum payable to the barrister originally appointed.

The amount to be paid to additional barristers appointed under the Revising Barristers Act, 1886, was, by sub-section two of section two of that Act, to be the sum of five guineas a day for every day that the barrister was employed, with three guineas a day for travelling and other expenses. This will now be limited to a maximum of 250 guineas in all.

Notes to Sect. 9.

The financial arrangements made by this section as regards the relative contributions of the Treasury and the county authorities will, of course, be subject to the passing of the Local Government Bill. In case the bill should not pass in time other provision is made under section eleven.

Perpetuation of 49 & 50 Vict. c. 42. Repeal of 6 & 7 Vict. c. 18, s. 59.

10.—(1.) Section four of the Revising Barristers Act, 1886, is hereby repealed, and that Act, as amended by this Act, shall be perpetual.

(2.) So long as a separate commission of assize is issued for the county of Surrey, that county shall be deemed to be a circuit within the meaning of section two, as well as of section one of the Revising Barristers Act, 1886.

(3.) An application to appoint an additional barrister under the said Act may be made at any time after the first day of September.

(4.) Section fifty-nine of the Parliamentary Voters Registration Act, 1843, is hereby repealed.

Enactments repealed by this section.

Section four of the Revising Barristers Act, 1886, provided for the continuance of that Act until the 31st December, 1887.

Applications to appoint additional barristers under that Act must before the alteration introduced by this section have been made at any time after the 5th September. These applications are made to a Secretary of State, and upon the Secretary notifying the fact to any judge of the High Court then sitting in chambers, the judge appoints the required number of duly qualified barristers.

Section fifty-nine of the Parliamentary Voters Registration Act, 1843 (6 & 7 Vict. c. 18), hereby repealed, provided

Notes to Sect. 10. for the remuneration of revising barristers as noted under the last preceding section. Part of it had been already repealed, viz., the part as to payment of additional barristers, by the Revising Barristers Act, 1874 (37 & 38 Vict. c. 53), and the remainder, as to payment out of the Consolidated Fund (which was superseded by 17 & 18 Vict. c. 94, providing for such payment out of moneys provided by Parliament for that purpose), was repealed by the Statute Law Revision Act, 1874 (37 & 38 Vict. c. 96).

Application of provisions of Act respecting county fund.

11.—(1.) In the event of a county authority being established under any Act of the present session, the provisions of this Act with respect to county authority, county, and county fund shall refer to the said county authority and to the county and county fund of such authority, and in case of any borough which, for the purposes of the said Act, is a county of itself, to the council of the borough and to the borough and borough fund.

(2.) In the event of a county authority not being established under any Act during the present session, the sums directed by this Act to be paid out of and into the county fund shall be paid by or under the direction of the local authority of every county quarter sessional area within the meaning of the Registration Act, 1885, in like manner as expenses or receipts of the clerk of the peace for such area under the Registration of Electors Acts, and by and under the direction of the council of every municipal borough which is also a parliamentary borough out of and into the borough fund,

48 & 49 Vict. c. 15.

and the amount to be paid for revising barristers shall be apportioned between such quarter sessional areas and boroughs upon the principles above mentioned in this Act. Sect. 11.

Sub-sect. 1.

The expressions "county authority," "county," and "county fund," as used in this sub-section, have already been explained in the notes to the preceding sections with reference to the Local Government Bill.

Sub-sect. 2. Meaning of "local authority."

The local authority of a county quarter sessional area, within the meaning of the Registration Act, 1885 (48 Vict. c. 15), is the court of county quarter sessions as defined by that Act.

By the nineteenth section of that Act, unless the context otherwise requires, the expression "court of county quarter sessions" means the justices in general or quarter sessions assembled for any county at large, or riding, or parts of a county at large, having a separate commission of the peace, and a separate court of quarter sessions, and includes the ustices in general or quarter sessions assembled for the Isle of Ely.

"County quarter sessional area."

The expression "county quarter sessional area" means the area of the jurisdiction as extended by this Act of any court of county quarter sessions, and includes the Isle of Ely; and save as aforesaid, for the purposes of this Act every liberty, county of a city, and county of a town, which for the purposes of parliamentary elections forms part of any county at large, riding, or parts, shall be deemed to be within the jurisdiction of the court of county quarter sessions and clerk of the peace of such county at large, riding, or parts.

"Clerk of the peace for such area."

The expression "clerk of the peace for a county quarter sessional area" means the clerk of the peace for such county at large, riding, or parts as aforesaid, and includes the clerk of the peace for the Isle of Ely.

Expenses and receipts of such clerk.

The expenses of the clerk of the peace for such an area are, by the fourteenth section of that Act, where such expenses were incurred partly in respect of a locality

Notes to Sect. 11. which does, and partly in respect of a locality (whether a division, liberty, county of a town, or other locality) which does not, contribute to the county rate levied by the court of county quarter sessions of such county quarter sessional area, to be apportioned by that court between the localities in the ratio, so nearly as may be, which the number of registered voters in each locality for the time being bear to each other, and the amount apportioned to any such non-contributing locality shall be defrayed out of the county rate, or rate in the nature of a county rate levied in such locality; and an order of the said court of county quarter sessions made on the treasurer, or other officer receiving such rate, shall be obeyed by and may be enforced against such treasurer, as if he were the treasurer of the court of county quarter sessions making the order.

The receipts of any clerk of the peace under the Parliamentary Registration Acts shall be applied in aid of the rate which bears the expenses of such clerk, and if there is more than one such rate, then of each rate in the proportion in which the expenses are borne by such rates.

Separate list of persons residing within fifteen miles of county.

12. A list of persons occupying property in a county, and residing within fifteen miles, but more than seven miles from the county, shall be made out in accordance with section forty-nine of the Municipal Corporations Act, 1882, and that section shall apply as if it were herein re-enacted, with the substitution of "county" for "borough," and of "county elector" for "burgess," and of "clerk of the peace" for "town clerk."

Section forty-nine of the Municipal Corporations Act, 1882 (45 & 46 Vict. c. 50), as applied by this section, will read as follows, viz.:

(1) The overseers of each parish shall, at the same time that they make the *parish county electors' list*, make

a list of the persons entitled in respect of the occupation of property in that parish to be elected *county councillors*, as being resident within fifteen miles, although beyond seven miles from the *county*.

Notes to Sect. 12.

(2) The provisions of this Act as applied to the *parish county electors' lists*, and claims and objections relating thereto, and the revision of those lists shall, as nearly as circumstances admit, apply to the lists made under this section (as applied).

(3) The clerk of the peace shall arrange the names entered in these lists, when revised, in alphabetical order as a separate list (in this Act (as applied) called the separate non-resident list), with an appropriate heading, at the end of the *county register*.

Qualification of councillors.

With this section must be read sections 11 and 12 of the Municipal Corporations Act, 1882 (45 & 46 Vict. c. 50), as applied under section two of the Local Government Bill, relating to the qualification of councillors.

Under section eleven, as applied, a person shall not be qualified to be elected or to be a councillor unless he—

(*a*) Is registered, or entitled to be registered, as *a county elector or* burgess ; or

(*b*) Being entitled to be so registered in all respects except that of residence, is resident beyond seven miles but within fifteen miles of the *county*, and entered in the separate non-resident list directed by *section twelve of the County Electors Act*, 1888, to be made ; and

(*c*) In either of those cases, is seised or possessed of real or personal property or both, to the value or amount, in the case of a *county* having four or more *electoral divisions*, of one thousand pounds, and in the case of any other *county*, of five hundred pounds, or is rated to the poor rate in the *county*, in the case of a *county* having four or more

Notes to Sect. 12.

electoral divisions, on the annual value of thirty pounds, and in the case of any other *county* of fifteen pounds.

Provided, that every person shall be qualified to be elected and to be a councillor who is, at the time of election, qualified to elect to the office of councillor; which last-mentioned qualification for being elected shall be alternative for and shall not repeal or take away any other qualification.

But if a person qualified under the last foregoing proviso ceases for six months to reside in the *county*, he shall cease to be qualified under that proviso, and his office shall become vacant, unless he was at the time of his election and continues to be qualified in some other manner.

Disqualification for being councillor.

Under section twelve as applied,

(1) A person shall be disqualified for being elected and for being a councillor, if and while he—

(*a*) Is an elective auditor [it is a question whether there will be any such office for the county], or holds any office or place of profit, other than that of *chairman* or sheriff, in the gift or disposal of the council; or

(*b*) Is in holy orders, or the regular minister of a dissenting congregation; or

(*c*) Has directly or indirectly, by himself or his partner, any share or interest in any contract or employment with, by, or on behalf of the council;

(2) But a person shall not be so disqualified or be deemed to have any share or interest in such a contract or employment by reason only of his having any share or interest in—

(*a*) Any lease, sale, or purchase of land or any agreement for the same; or

(*b*) Any agreement for the loan of money, or any security for the payment of money only; or

(*c*) Any newspaper in which any advertisement relating to the affairs of the *county* or council is inserted; or (*d*) Any company which contracts with the council for lighting or supplying with water or insuring against fire any part of the *county;* or

(*e*) Any railway company, or any company incorporated by Act of Parliament or Royal Charter or under the Companies Act, 1862.

Notes to Sect. 12.

Precepts by clerk of the peace.

13. All precepts, notices, and forms required for the purposes of the Registration of Electors Acts shall be altered in such manner as may be declared by Her Majesty in Council to be necessary for carrying into effect this Act, and clerks of the peace and town clerks shall alter their precepts and forms accordingly, and if clerks of the peace or town clerks have sent out precepts to the overseers before the passing of this Act, they shall send to them such supplemental precepts as are necessary or desirable for instructing them to carry into effect this Act.

Precepts, notices, and forms under this section are to be issued as provided.

A calendar of things to be done in order of date under this Act in the current year is prefixed to this book, and will, it is hoped, be found of practical utility to all concerned in carrying into effect the provisions of the Act.

Definitions.

14. In this Act, unless the context otherwise requires,—

The expressions "urban district" and "rural district" respectively mean an urban or rural sanitary district, also any urban or rural district under any Act of the present session of Parliament;

Sect. 13. The expression "clerk of the peace" means, in the event of the establishment of a county authority, the person acting as clerk of that authority, and such person shall act as clerk of the peace throughout the whole county of such authority, both for the purposes of this Act and of the Registration of Electors Acts; subject nevertheless—

(*a*) to the provisions of the Registration Act, 1885, respecting the case of any parliamentary county extending into more county quarter sessional areas than one, and

(*b*) to the proviso that where at the passing of this Act any clerk of the peace acts as clerk of the peace under the Registration of Electors Acts he shall continue so to act, but shall act as deputy of the person acting as clerk of the peace by virtue of this Act.

In determining the electoral divisions for the first election of county councillors under the Local Government Bill, every urban sanitary district and rural sanitary district existing at the date of such first election is to be a county district, and where a rural sanitary district is situate in more than one county, then each portion of such district which is situate on either side the boundary is to be a separate county district in the county in which it is situate. (L. G. B. sect. 52.)

The clerk of the peace for the county is, under section eighty-two of the Local Government Bill, to be the clerk of the county council, and is when acting under the Acts relating to the registration of parliamentary voters to act under the direction of the county council.

Notes to Sect. 13.

The provisions of the Registration Act, 1885 (48 Vict. c. 15), respecting the case of any parliamentary county extending into more county quarter-sessional areas than one, herein referred to, are contained in section seven, sub-section three, of that Act, which provides that, in such case, the clerk of the peace of each county quarter sessional area shall, in respect of each parish in such parliamentary county which is within his jurisdiction, act as and be deemed to be the clerk of the peace of the county within the meaning of the Parliamentary Registration Acts and this Act, until the lists of voters for such parish have been revised; but the revising barrister shall transmit the revised lists of voters for such parish to the clerk of the peace of the county quarter sessional area which comprises the largest part in extent of the said parliamentary county, and, save as aforesaid, such last-mentioned clerk shall, as respects the said parliamentary county, act as and be deemed to be sole clerk of the peace of the county for the purposes of the Parliamentary Registration Acts and this Act.

Transitory provisions as to the year 1888.

15. In the year one thousand eight hundred and eighty-eight, notwithstanding anything in this Act or the enactments applied by this Act, the revision of the lists of parliamentary voters and county electors may be later than the twelfth day of October, so that it be not later than the thirty-first day of October, and the register of county electors shall be completed on or before the thirty-first day of December in the said year, and shall come into operation on the first day of January, one thousand eight hundred and eighty-nine, and

Sect. 15. shall continue in operation until the next register of county electors comes into operation.

In the year one thousand eight hundred and eighty-eight, notwithstanding anything in this Act or the enactments thereby applied, the clerk of the peace in a county may, if he thinks fit, instead of directing the occupiers' list to be made out in three divisions as provided by the Registration of Electors Acts, direct the overseers to make supplemental lists containing the names which would otherwise be contained in division two and division three of the occupiers' list respectively, and the names so contained in the supplemental list corresponding to division two shall be struck by the revising barrister out of division one of the list, and the supplemental list corresponding to division two or division three shall be treated as if it were division two or three of the said list, as the case may be.

As to the time for appealing, see, however, the notes to section six, sub-section two, of this Act.

As to lists made out in divisions, see *ante*, pp. 26 and 27, in the notes to section four of this Act.

SCHEDULE.

Registration Act, 1885.

Definition of Ten Pounds Occupation Qualification. **Sect. 3.**

Ten pounds occupation qualification.

A person entitled to be registered as a voter in respect of a ten pounds occupation qualification in a borough, municipal or parliamentary—

(*a*) Must during the whole twelve months immediately preceding the fifteenth day of July have been an occupier as owner or tenant of some land or tenement in a parish [or township] of the clear yearly value of not less than ten pounds ; and

(*b*) Must have resided in or within seven miles of the borough during six months immediately preceding the fifteenth day of July ; and

(*c*) Such person, or some one else, must during the said twelve months have been rated to all poor rates made in respect of such land or tenement ; and

(*d*) All sums due in respect of the said land or tenement on account of any poor rate made and allowed during the twelve months immediately preceding the fifth day of January next before the registration, or on account of any assessed taxes due before the said fifth day of January, must have been paid on or before the twentieth day of July.

If two or more persons jointly are such occupiers as above mentioned, and the value of the land or tenement is such as to give ten pounds or more for each occupier, each of such occupiers is entitled to be registered as a voter.

If a person has occupied in the borough different lands or tenements of the requisite value in immediate succession during the said twelve months, he is entitled in respect of the occupation thereof to be registered as a voter in the parish [or township] in which the last occupied land or tenement is situate.

APPENDIX.

AN ACT to provide for the Qualification and Registration of Electors for the purposes of Local Government in England and Wales. [16th May, 1888.]

WHEREAS it is expedient to make provision with respect to the qualification and registration of electors of any representative bodies (in this Act referred to as "county authorities") which may be established under any Act of the present session of Parliament for the purposes of local government in counties in England.

Be it therefore enacted by the Queen's most Excellent Majesty, by and with the advice and consent of the Lords Spiritual and Temporal, and Commons, in this present Parliament assembled, and by the authority of the same, as follows:

1. This Act may be cited as the County Electors Act, 1888. Short title and construction.

The Registration Act, 1885, and the Parliamentary Registration Acts within the meaning of that Act, are in this Act referred to as the Registration of Electors Acts, and together with this Act may be cited as the Registration of Electors Acts, 1843 to 1888. 48 & 49 Vict. c. 15.

Sect. 1. This Act shall be construed as one with the Registration of Electors Acts.

Extension of burgess franchise to county electors outside municipal boroughs. 45 & 46 Vict. c. 50.

2. (1.) For the purpose of the election of county authorities in England, the burgess qualification, that is to say, the qualification enacted by section nine of the Municipal Corporations Act, 1882, shall extend to every part of a county not within the limits of a borough, and a person possessing in any part of a county outside the limits of a borough such burgess qualification, shall be entitled to be registered under this Act as a county elector in the parish in which the qualifying property is situate.

(2.) Sections nine, thirty-one, thirty-three, and sixty-three of the Municipal Corporations Act, 1882, and any enactments of that or any other Act affecting the same, shall extend to so much of every county as is not comprised within the limits of a municipal borough in like manner as if they were herein re-enacted, with the substitution of "county" for "borough" and of "county elector" for "burgess," and with the other necessary modifications.

Occupation of land of the value of 10*l.* to qualify.

3. Every person who is entitled to be registered as a voter in respect of a ten pounds occupation qualification within the meaning of the provisions of the Registration Act, 1885, which are set out in the schedule to this Act, shall be entitled to be registered as a county elector, and to be enrolled as a burgess, in respect of such qualification, in like manner in all respects as if the sections of the Municipal Corporations

Act, 1882, relating to a burgess qualification included the said ten pounds occupation qualification. **Sect. 3.**

4. (1.) The Registration of Electors Acts shall, so far as circumstances admit, apply to the enrolment of burgesses in a municipal borough to which the Parliamentary and Municipal Registration Act, 1878, does not apply, and to the registration of county electors within the meaning of this Act; and the lists of burgesses, and of county electors, and of occupation voters for parliamentary elections, shall, so far as practicable, be made out and revised together; and the Registration of Electors Acts shall accordingly— Registration of county electors. 41 & 42 Vict. c. 26.

(*a*) apply to every such municipal borough in like manner as if it were a borough to which sub-section two of section six of the Registration Act, 1885, applied (sub-section one of which section is hereby repealed), and revising assessors for such borough shall not be elected; and

(*b*) apply to every parish not situate in a municipal borough, in like manner as if such parish were a municipal borough to which the Parliamentary and Municipal Registration Act, 1878, applies, and the said lists of county electors and of occupation voters for parliamentary elections in such parish shall be made out in divisions, as provided in the said Act: Provided that a person whose name appears in any list of county electors or bur-

Sect. 4.

gesses in a county may object to the name of any other person on a list of county electors or burgesses for a parish in that county, and may oppose the claim of a person to have his name inscribed in any such list.

(2.) In the construction of the Registration of Electors Acts for the purpose of their application to a parish not situate in a municipal borough, there shall be made the variations following, and such other variations as may be necessary for carrying into effect the application, that is to say:—

(*a*) Where such parish is not within a parliamentary borough, "parliamentary county" shall be substituted for "parliamentary borough;"

(*b*) Where such parish is not within a parliamentary borough, the clerk of the peace shall perform the duties of and be substituted for the town clerk; but any notice required to be given to the town clerk by section twenty-seven of the Parliamentary and Municipal Registration Act, 1878, relating to the withdrawal and revival of objections, shall be given to the overseers and not to the clerk of the peace;

(*c*) County elector shall be substituted for burgess;

(*d*) Section nine of the Parliamentary and Municipal Registration Act, 1878, shall not apply to any parish which is not wholly situate in an urban district;

(*e*) Where such parish is not within a parliamentary borough section twenty-one of the Parliamentary and Municipal Registration Act, 1878, shall not apply, and the lists and register of voters shall be made out alphabetically, but shall be framed in parts for polling districts and electoral divisions and for urban districts and for wards of urban and rural districts in such a manner that the parts may be conveniently compiled or put together to serve as lists for polling districts, and elections in urban districts and as electoral division or ward lists; Sect. 4.

(*f*) Where such parish is within a parliamentary borough—

(i.) the overseers shall send to the clerk of the peace for the county two copies of the lists of voters at the same time at which they send copies to the town clerk; and

(ii.) the town clerk shall cause to be printed such number of copies of the revised lists as the clerk of the peace may require, and shall transmit the same to the clerk of the peace, who shall deal with the same as with other lists of county electors in his county; but,

(iii.) save as aforesaid, the clerk of the peace shall not act in relation to

Sect. 4.

the registration of county electors in the said parish, and the town clerk of the parliamentary borough shall be the town clerk within the meaning of the Registration of Electors Acts and this Act in relation to such parish, and shall include in his precept to the overseers proper directions respecting the registration of the county electors within the meaning of this Act.

(*g*) The lists of occupation voters and county electors shall be revised by the revising barrister for the parliamentary borough or county in which such parish is situate, and the revising barrister for revising the county electors' lists for the whole or any part of an electoral division of any county shall, if so required by the county council, hold a court in that electoral division or at some convenient place in a division adjoining thereto.

(*h*) The guardians of a union which is not wholly comprised in an urban district may, with the consent of the overseers of any parish or parishes within their union for which an assistant overseer has not been appointed, annually appoint a fit person to act as registration officer for such parish or parishes, and may remove any such person, and fill up any vacancy caused by death, resignation, or otherwise. Such registration officer shall perform all the duties of overseers of the parish or parishes for which he is appointed in respect of the registration of county electors and parliamentary voters, and the provisions of the Registration of Electors Acts relating to overseers, including those providing for penalties, shall apply to him accordingly: Sect. 4.

Provided that his remuneration shall be fixed and paid by the guardians of the union, and charged on the poor rates of the parish or parishes for which he is appointed, and (if he acts for more than one parish) in proportion to the number of persons on the registers made during the year of his appointment of county electors and parliamentary voters for each parish.

(3.) Notwithstanding anything in this Act contained, where a municipal borough or an urban district is co-extensive with any electoral division or divisions of a parliamentary county, the lists of voters may be directed by the county authority to be made out according to the order in which the qualifying premises appear in the rate book, and section twenty-one of the Parliamentary and Municipal Registration Act, 1878, shall apply to such borough or urban district, and where lists of voters are so made out nothing in this

Sect. 4. Act shall require such part of the county register as consists of these lists to be arranged alphabetically.

Making out of lists and registers in metropolis.

5. After the year one thousand eight hundred and eighty-eight, in every part of the metropolis, and in every part of a parliamentary borough, the whole or greater part of which is situate in the metropolis, the lists and registers of parliamentary voters, and of county electors, shall, unless the local authority otherwise direct, be arranged in the same order in which the qualifying premises appear in the rate book for the parish in which those premises are situate, or as nearly thereto as will cause those lists and registers to record the qualifying premises in successive order in the street or other place in which they are situate.

For the purpose of this section "metropolis" means the city of London and the parishes and places mentioned in Schedules (A.), (B.), and (C.) of the Metropolis Management Act, 1855.

18 & 19 Vict. c. 120.

Revision of electoral lists.

6. (1.) The lists of parliamentary voters, and of burgesses, and of county electors, shall be revised between the eighth day of September and the twelfth day of October both inclusive, and shall be revised as soon as possible after the seventh day of September, and the eighth day of September shall be substituted in the Acts relating to the registration of parliamentary voters for the fifteenth day of September; and the declarations under section ten of the County Voters Registration Act, 1865, and section twenty-four of the

28 & 29 Vict. c. 36.

Parliamentary and Municipal Registration Act, 1878, shall be sent to the clerk of the peace or town clerk on or before the fifth day of September.

Sect. 6.

41 & 42 Vict. c. 26.

(2.) In sections sixty-two and sixty-three of the Parliamentary Voters Registration Act, 1843 (relating to appeals from revising barristers in England), "the Michaelmas sittings of the High Court of Justice" shall be substituted for "the Michaelmas term," and forthwith after the fourth day of the Michaelmas sittings a court or courts shall sit for the purpose of hearing such appeals, and those appeals shall be heard and determined continuously and without delay, and any statement by the barrister for the purpose of any such appeal made in pursuance of section forty-two of the said Act may be made at any time within ten days after the conclusion of the revision, so that it be made not less than four days before the first day of the said Michaelmas sittings, and the statement need not be read in open court, but shall be submitted to the appellant, who, if he approves the same, shall sign the same as directed by the said section, and return the same to the barrister.

6 & 7 Vict. c. 18.

Roll of county electors.

7. (1.) The clerk of the peace of every county shall make up a register of all persons registered as burgesses or county electors in the county, both for the county and for each electoral division into which the county is divided for the purpose of election of the county authority, and such number of copies as the clerk of the peace may require of the list of burgesses as revised

Sect. 7. shall be delivered by the town clerk to such clerk of the peace for the purpose of making up such register.

(2.) The Registration of Electors Acts, and sections forty-five, forty-eight, and seventy-one of the Municipal Corporations Act, 1882, shall apply, for the purposes of this section, with the substitution of clerk of the peace for town clerk, and of county register and division register for burgess roll and ward roll respectively, and of electoral division for ward, and of county fund for borough fund.

45 & 46 Vict. c. 50.

(3.) If district councils are established under any Act of the present session of Parliament, the clerk of every such council, not being the council of a borough, shall make up a register of all persons registered as county electors in his district, and where there are wards in a district, of all county electors in each ward, and he shall obtain from the clerk of the peace a sufficient number of copies of the lists of the county electors so registered as may be required for the purpose of making up such register and supplying the same to the public, and the above-mentioned Acts and sections shall apply for that purpose, with the substitution of "clerk of the district council" for "town clerk," and of "district register" for "burgess roll" respectively;

(4.) Provided that nothing in this section shall prevent a county elector from being registered in more than one division register.

48 & 49 Vict. c. 15.

(5.) Where in pursuance of section four of the Registration Act, 1885, the revising barrister has power to

Sect. 7.

erase the name of any person as a parliamentary voter from division one of the occupiers' list, such barrister, in lieu of erasing the name, shall place an asterisk or other mark against the name, and, in printing such lists, the name shall be numbered consecutively with the other names, but an asterisk or other mark shall be printed against the name, and a person against whose name such asterisk or other mark is placed shall not be entitled to vote in respect of such entry at a parliamentary election, but shall have the same right of voting at an election of a county authority as he would have if no such mark were placed against his name.

(6.) If under any Act of the present session of Parliament establishing a council for a county any portion of another county is added to that county for the purpose of such election, such portion of the county register as relates to the electors having qualifying property in the said part so added shall be deemed to be part of the county register of the county for which such council is elected, and the clerk of the peace and other officers shall take such steps as may be necessary for giving effect to these enactments.

Expenses.

8.—(1.) All expenses properly incurred and all sums received in carrying into effect the provisions of this Act and the Registration of Electors Acts with respect to county electors,—

(*a*) if incurred or received by overseers, shall be respectively paid and applied as expenses and receipts of overseers under the Regis-

Sect. 8.

tration of Electors Acts in the case of the lists of parliamentary voters; and

(b) if incurred or received by the clerk of the peace or town clerk, shall be paid out of or into the county or borough fund; and such expenses shall include all proper and reasonable fees and charges made and charged by him for the trouble, care, and attention of such clerk in the performance of the services and duties imposed on him by the said provisions.

Remuneration of revising barristers and contribution by county authorities.

9. Every barrister appointed to revise any list of voters under the Parliamentary Voters Registration Act, 1843, shall be paid the sum of two hundred and fifty guineas by way of remuneration to him, and in satisfaction of his travelling and other expenses, and every such barrister, after the termination of his last sitting, shall forward his appointment to the Commissioners of Her Majesty's Treasury, who shall make an order for the payment of the above sum to every such barrister.

49 & 50 Vict. c. 42.

The maximum amount to be paid to an additional barrister in pursuance of the Revising Barristers Act, 1886, shall not exceed the amount authorised by this section to be paid to a revising barrister.

The sums so paid to a revising barrister or an assistant barrister shall be payable partly out of moneys provided by Parliament and partly by the county authorities, as hereinafter mentioned.

Sect. 9.

(1.) There shall be annually paid by the county authority of every county out of the county fund into Her Majesty's Exchequer such sum as the Treasury certify to be one-half of the cost incurred for the payment of revising barristers at the then last revision of the lists of parliamentary electors, burgesses, and county electors in that county.

(2.) The Treasury shall yearly ascertain the total cost of the revising barristers appointed for all the counties and boroughs on any circuit, and shall divide one-half of such cost among the counties comprised in such circuit in proportion to the number of burgesses and county electors in each county, and certify the amount which under such apportionment is due under this section from each county. The Treasury may vary such certificate if they think fit, but unless it is so varied the certificate shall be final.

(3.) So much of any Act as requires a payment out of the borough fund of any borough to a revising barrister, in respect of the revision of the burgess lists, shall be repealed, without prejudice to any payment or liability previously made or incurred.

10.—(1.) Section four of the Revising Barristers Act, 1886, is hereby repealed, and that Act, as amended by this Act, shall be perpetual. Perpetuation of 49 & 50 Vict. c. 42

Sect. 10.

Repeal of 6 & 7 Vict. c. 18, s. 59.

(2.) So long as a separate commission of assize is issued for the county of Surrey, that county shall be deemed to be a circuit within the meaning of section two, as well as of section one of the Revising Barristers Act, 1886.

(3.) An application to appoint an additional barrister under the said Act may be made at any time after the first day of September.

(4.) Section fifty-nine of the Parliamentary Voters Registration Act, 1843, is hereby repealed.

Application of provisions of Act respecting county fund.

11.—(1.) In the event of a county authority being established under any Act of the present session, the provisions of this Act with respect to county authority, county, and county fund shall refer to the said county authority and to the county and county fund of such authority, and in case of any borough which, for the purposes of the said Act, is a county of itself, to the council of the borough and to the borough and borough fund.

(2.) In the event of a county authority not being established under any Act during the present session, the sums directed by this Act to be paid out of and into the county fund shall be paid by or under the direction of the local authority of every county quarter sessional area within the meaning of the Registration Act, 1885, in like manner as expenses or receipts of the clerk of the peace for such area under the Registration of Electors Acts, and by and under the direction of the council of every municipal borough

48 & 49 Vict. c. 15.

which is also a parliamentary borough out of and into the borough fund, and the amount to be paid for revising barristers shall be apportioned between such quarter sessional areas and boroughs upon the principles above mentioned in this Act. **Sect. 11.**

12. A list of persons occupying property in a county, and residing within fifteen miles, but more than seven miles from the county, shall be made out in accordance with section forty-nine of the Municipal Corporations Act, 1882, and that section shall apply as if it were herein re-enacted, with the substitution of "county" for "borough," and of "county elector" for "burgess," and of "clerk of the peace" for "town clerk." **Separate list of persons residing within fifteen miles of county.**

13. All precepts, notices, and forms required for the purposes of the Registration of Electors Acts shall be altered in such manner as may be declared by Her Majesty in Council to be necessary for carrying into effect this Act, and clerks of the peace and town clerks shall alter their precepts and forms accordingly, and if clerks of the peace or town clerks have sent out precepts to the overseers before the passing of this Act, they shall send to them such supplemental precepts as are necessary or desirable for instructing them to carry into effect this Act. **Precepts by clerk of the peace.**

14. In this Act, unless the context otherwise requires,— **Definitions.**

The expressions "urban district" and "rural district" respectively mean an urban or rural sani-

Sect. 14.

tary district, also any urban or rural district under any Act of the present session of Parliament;

The expression "clerk of the peace" means, in the event of the establishment of a county authority, the person acting as clerk of that authority, and such person shall act as clerk of the peace throughout the whole county of such authority, both for the purposes of this Act and of the Registration of Electors Acts; subject nevertheless—

(*a*) to the provisions of the Registration Act, 1885, respecting the case of any parliamentary county extending into more county quarter sessional areas than one, and

(*b*) to the proviso that where at the passing of this Act any clerk of the peace acts as clerk of the peace under the Registration of Electors Acts he shall continue so to act, but shall act as deputy of the person acting as clerk of the peace by virtue of this Act.

Transitory provisions as to the year 1888.

15. In the year one thousand eight hundred and eighty-eight, notwithstanding anything in this Act or the enactments applied by this Act, the revision of the lists of parliamentary voters and county electors may be later than the twelfth day of October, so that it be not later than the thirty-first day of October, and the register of county electors shall be completed on or before the thirty-first day of December in the said year, and shall come into operation on the first day of

January, one thousand eight hundred and eighty-nine, and shall continue in operation until the next register of county electors comes into operation. Sect. 15.

In the year one thousand eight hundred and eighty-eight, notwithstanding anything in this Act or the enactments thereby applied, the clerk of the peace in a county may, if he thinks fit, instead of directing the occupiers' list to be made out in three divisions as provided by the Registration of Electors Acts, direct the overseers to make supplemental lists containing the names which would otherwise be contained in division two and division three of the occupiers' list respectively, and the names so contained in the supplemental list corresponding to division two shall be struck by the revising barrister out of division one of the list, and the supplemental list corresponding to division two or division three shall be treated as if it were division two or three of the said list, as the case may be.

SCHEDULE.

Registration Act, 1885.

Sect. 3. *Definition of Ten Pounds Occupation Qualification.*

Ten pounds occupation qualification.

A person entitled to be registered as a voter in respect of a ten pounds occupation qualification in a borough, municipal or parliamentary—

(*a*) must during the whole twelve months immediately preceding the fifteenth day of July have been an occupier as owner or tenant of some land or tenement in a parish [or township] of the clear yearly value of not less than ten pounds; and

(*b*) must have resided in or within seven miles of the borough during six months immediately preceding the fifteenth day of July; and

(*c*) such person, or some one else, must during the said twelve months have been rated to all poor rates made in respect of such land or tenement; and

(*d*) all sums due in respect of the said land or tenement on account of any poor rate made and allowed during the twelve months immediately preceding the fifth day of January next before the registration, or on account of any assessed taxes due before the said fifth day of January, must have been paid on or before the twentieth day of July.

If two or more persons jointly are such occupiers as above mentioned, and the value of the land or tenement is such as to give ten pounds or more for each occupier, each of such occupiers is entitled to be registered as a voter.

If a person has occupied in the borough different lands or tenements of the requisite value in immediate succession during the said twelve months, he is entitled in respect of the occupation thereof to be registered as a voter in the parish [or township] in which the last occupied land or tenement is situate.

APPENDIX II.

NOTE ON THE SUPPLEMENTAL PRECEPTS AND FORMS FOR THE YEAR 1888.

Note to Precepts.

THERE has been some delay in the issue of the Supplemental Precepts and Forms for the current year under section thirteen of the Act, which has retarded the publication of this book, as it was felt that the practical value of any edition of the Act without those Precepts and Forms would be seriously lessened. Now, however, that those Precepts and Forms have at length been prepared and issued, a few remarks upon them seem to be necessary.

It is to be observed that these Precepts and Forms are not issued as sanctioned by any Order in Council under section thirteen of the Act, but derive whatever authority they may possess in relation to their use by Town Clerks and Clerks of the Peace, as being prepared and issued by and at the instance of the Local Government Board, which has never before intervened in such matters, but which will be under the provisions of the Local Government Bill intimately concerned in the settlement of the boundaries of local government areas.

In all the Supplemental Precepts alike no notice has been taken of the fact that a ten pounds burgess occupier will not be entitled to be registered as a county elector or enrolled as a burgess unless he has, on or before the 20th July next, paid all sums on account of assessed taxes due before the fifth of January last.

Note to Precepts.

This is of small importance as regards the registration of ten pounds burgess occupiers in parliamentary or merged parliamentary boroughs, because there the same thing is required of parliamentary ten pounds occupiers, nor will it matter in any case where the subject-matter of a ten pounds burgess occupation qualification consists of land only, for the inhabited house duty is the only kind of assessed tax the non-payment of which will now disqualify. But it is as well to remember that a house may be the subject-matter of a ten pounds occupation qualification as well as land, and that many persons may, no doubt, claim to be registered as county electors or burgesses in respect of houses of sufficient value in which they may have resided only six months, or in respect of which they may possibly not have paid county rates, in which cases they will not be qualified unless they have paid the inhabited house duty.

The Supplemental Precept of the Clerk of the Peace has a note appended to it upon its application to parishes in municipal boroughs to which the Parliamentary and Municipal Registration Act, 1878, does not apply. This note seems hardly sufficient to meet the case. By sub-section (1) (*a*) of section 4 of the Act the Registration of Electors Acts are to apply to every such municipal borough in like manner as if it were a borough to which sub-section two of section six of the Registration Act, 1885, applied (sub-section one of which section is hereby repealed). Sub-section two of section six of that Act (as noted in the notes to section four) enacts that the Parliamentary and Municipal Registration Act, 1878, shall apply to such municipal borough, subject nevertheless (*inter alia*) to paragraph (*c*), whereby "The overseers of every parish in such municipal borough shall send to the clerk of the peace for the parliamentary county two copies of the lists

Note to Precepts.

of voters at the same time at which they send copies to the town clerk, and the lists of voters for a parish in such borough, when revised, shall be transmitted by the revising barrister to such clerk of the peace, and dealt with by him as with other lists in his county; but, save as aforesaid, the town clerk of the municipal borough shall, until such transmission, act as and be deemed to be the town clerk within the meaning of the Parliamentary Registration Acts and this Act in relation to such parish, and the clerk of the peace shall not act in relation to the registration of occupation voters in such parish."

This seems to make it necessary for the town clerk of such municipal borough to issue the necessary supplemental precept, and expressly to forbid the clerk of the peace for the parliamentary county to do so. If the clerk of the peace, however, does in fact do so, probably the lists of voters will not be invalidated thereby; but the expenses of the clerk of the peace in relation thereto ought, so it seems, to be disallowed, because under sections eight and eleven of the Act these expenses ought to fall on the borough fund, and not upon the county.

Moreover, the overseers are not directed by this precept to make out a list of persons entitled to be elected councillors and aldermen of such municipal borough, though not entitled to be on the burgess roll thereof, because they have been resident beyond seven miles though within fifteen miles of such municipal borough. It seems that the overseers ought to do this, because the Local Government Bill, even if it does pass this year, does not apparently, at least in its present form, abolish altogether the municipal council of any such small borough.

The forms, also, when used for the purposes of the registration of occupation voters and burgesses in such a municipal borough, will require careful handling; for instance, the

Note to Precepts.

forms of notices as to rates appended to the Supplemental Precept of the Town Clerk, Form B., would be much more easily adjusted to such use than the forms of notices as to rates appended to the Supplemental Precept of the Clerk of the Peace.

As to the Supplemental Precepts to be issued by the Town Clerk, Form A. omits all mention of any list of persons entitled to be on the list of persons entitled to be county councillors though not entitled to be on the burgess roll, because not resident within seven miles of the borough though resident within fifteen miles of the county. It is quite conceivable that such a list may be wanted, for there may be a parish situated within a municipal and within a parliamentary borough, and at the same time situate also within the county of a council under the Local Government Bill. The boundaries of counties of councils under that Bill are given in the notes to section 2 of the Act.

The Supplemental Precept of the Town Clerk, Form B., does not appear to call for any further remark.

FORM OF SUPPLEMENTAL PRECEPT OF THE CLERK OF THE PEACE TO THE OVERSEERS IN THE YEAR 1888.

Precept by Clerk of Peace

REGISTRATION OF PARLIAMENTARY VOTERS AND COUNTY ELECTORS.

County of } To the overseers of the poor of the parish of
to wit. } . [*or* of the township of].

IN pursuance of the provisions of the County Electors Act, 1888, I require your attention to the following instructions respecting the registration of parliamentary voters and county electors.

This precept is supplemental to my former precept which I sent you in April last.

---

1. In this precept the expression "county electors" means persons entitled to be registered in respect of the old burgess qualification or of the ten pounds occupation burgess qualification.

2. A county elector may be a man or a woman, but must be of full age and not subject to any legal incapacity, and must not at any time within the twelve months next before the fifteenth day of July next have received any parochial relief; but where a person has received for himself or for any member of his family any medical or surgical assistance, or any medicine, at the expense of any poor rate, he is not thereby deprived of his right to be registered.

County electors;

Precept by Clerk of Peace.

Old burgess qualification.

3. A person entitled to be registered as a county elector in respect of the old burgess qualification—

(*a*) must during the whole of the twelve months immediately preceding the fifteenth day of July next have been an occupier of a house, warehouse, counting-house, shop, or other building in your parish [*or* township]; and

(*b*) must have resided during those twelve months in the county or within seven miles thereof; and

(*c*) such person or some one else must during the said twelve months have been rated to all poor rates made in respect of the qualifying property; and

(*d*) all sums due in respect of the qualifying property on account of any poor rate made and allowed, during the twelve months immediately preceding the fifth day of January last, must have been paid on or before the twentieth day of July next; and

(*e*) if the county rate is not levied with the poor rate all sums due in respect of the qualifying property on account of any county rate made during the twelve months immediately preceding the fifth day of January last must have been paid on or before the twentieth day of July next.

A person is entitled to be registered in respect of the old burgess qualification notwithstanding that he has permitted his dwelling-house to be occupied as a furnished house for a time not exceeding four months, and during that time has not resided as above mentioned.

If two or more persons are joint occupiers of property qualifying for the old burgess qualification, each such occupier is entitled to be registered.

Precept by Clerk of Peace.

Ten pounds occupation burgess qualification.

4. A person entitled to be registered as a county elector in respect of the ten pounds occupation burgess qualification—

(*a*) must during the whole twelve months immediately preceding the fifteenth day of July have been an occupier as owner or tenant of some land or tenement in your parish [*or* township] of the clear yearly value of not less than ten pounds; and

(*b*) must have resided in or within seven miles of the county during six months immediately preceding the fifteenth day of July next; and

(*c*) such person, or some one else, must during the said twelve months have been rated to all poor rates made in respect of such land or tenement; and

(*d*) all sums due in respect of the said land or tenement on account of any poor rate made and allowed during the twelve months immediately preceding the fifth day of January last, must have been paid on or before the twentieth day of July next.

If two or more persons jointly are such occupiers as above mentioned, and the value of the land or tenement is such as to give ten pounds or more for each occupier, each of such occupiers is entitled to be registered as a voter.

5. If a person has occupied in immediate succession during the said twelve months different premises in the county which would qualify him for registration as a county elector, he is entitled, in respect of the occupation thereof, to be registered as a county elector in the parish [*or* township] in which the last occupied premises are situate.

Qualification of councillors.

6. A person who is entitled to be registered as a county elector in all respects except that of residence, and is resi-

Precept by Clerk of Peace.

dent beyond seven miles, but within fifteen miles, of the said county, is entitled to be on the list of persons entitled to be elected councillors though not entitled to be on the county register.

Parliamentary occupation voters.

7. In this precept the expression "parliamentary occupation voters" means persons entitled to be registered as parliamentary voters in respect of,—

(*a.*) a fifty pounds rental qualification as hereafter defined in paragraph 9 of this precept;

(*b.*) a ten pounds occupation qualification as hereafter defined in paragraph 10 of this precept; or

(*c.*) a household qualification as hereafter defined in paragraph 11 of this precept; or

(*d.*) A lodger qualification as hereafter defined in paragraph 12 of this precept.

General qualification.

8. Every person entitled to be registered as a parliamentary occupation voter must be a man of full age and not subject to any legal incapacity, and must not at any time during the twelve months immediately preceding the fifteenth day of July next have received any parochial relief, but where a person has received for himself or for any member of his family any medical or surgical assistance, or any medicine, at the expense of any poor rate, he is not thereby deprived of his right to be registered.

Fifty pounds rental qualification.

9. A person entitled to be registered as a parliamentary voter in respect of a fifty pounds rental qualification—

(*a.*) must on the fifteenth day of July next be an occupier as tenant of some land or tenement for which he is *bonâ fide* liable to a yearly rent of not less than fifty pounds; and

(*b.*) must have occupied such land or tenement for the whole of the twelve months immediately preceding the fifteenth day of July next; and (*c.*) must have been registered as a voter in respect of the said occupation in the register of voters in force during the year one thousand eight hundred and eighty-four.

Precept by Clerk of Peace.

If two or more persons jointly are such occupiers as above mentioned, and the rent is such as to give fifty pounds or more for each occupier, each such occupier, if he was registered in respect of the said occupation as aforesaid in the year one thousand eight hundred and eighty-four, is entitled to be registered as a parliamentary voter.

Ten pounds occupation qualification.

10. A person entitled to be registered as a parliamentary voter in respect of a ten pounds occupation qualification—

(*a*) must on the fifteenth day of July next be, and during the whole twelve months immediately preceding that day have been, an occupier, as owner or tenant, of some land or tenement in your parish [*or* township] of the clear yearly value of not less than ten pounds; and

(*b*) such person, or someone else, must during those twelve months have been rated to all poor rates made in respect of such land or tenement; and

(*c*) all sums due in respect of the said land or tenement on account of any poor rate made and allowed during the twelve months immediately preceding the fifth day of January last must have been paid on or before the twentieth day of July next.

If two or more persons, jointly, are such occupiers as above mentioned, and the clear yearly value of the land or tenement is such as to give ten pounds or more for each occupier, two of such occupiers are entitled to be registered as parliamentary voters; but no more are so entitled (unless they derived the property by descent, succession,

Schedule 2. Sec 30 & 31

Precept by Clerk of Peace.

Vict. c. 102, s. 27.

marriage, marriage settlement, or devise, or) unless they are *boná fide* engaged as partners carrying on trade or business thereon, in any of which cases all may be registered, if the clear yearly value is sufficient to give ten pounds for each occupier.

If a person has occupied different lands or tenements in your divison [*or* county] of the requisite value in immediate succession during the said twelve months he is entitled in respect of the occupation thereof to be registered as a parliamentary voter in the parish [*or* township] in which the last occupied land or tenement is situate.

Household qualification.

11. A person entitled to be registered as a parliamentary voter in respect of a household qualification--

(*a*) must on the fifteenth day of July next be, and for the whole twelve months immediately preceding that day (except the time (if any) not exceeding four months during which he has permitted the house to be occupied as a furnished house), have been, an inhabitant occupier of some dwelling-house in your parish [*or* township], or of some part of a house separately occupied as a dwelling; and

(*b*) such person or someone else must during those twelve months have been rated to all poor rates made in respect of the said dwelling-house; and

(*c*) all sums due in respect of the said dwelling-house on account of any poor rate made and allowed during the twelve months immediately preceding the fifth day of January last must have been paid on or before the twentieth day of July next.

If two or more persons are joint occupiers of a dwelling-house no one of them is entitled to be registered as a parliamentary voter in respect of a household qualification in respect thereof, though if the value is sufficient, one or more of them may be entitled under paragraph 10 above.

Precept by Clerk of Peace.

If a person has occupied different dwelling-houses in your division [*or* county] in immediate succession during the said twelve months he is entitled in respect of the occupation thereof to be registered as a parliamentary voter in the parish [*or* township] in which the last occupied dwelling-house is situate.

If a person inhabits a dwelling-house by virtue of any office, service, or employment, and the dwelling-house is not inhabited by any person under whom such man serves in such office, service, or employment, he is to be considered as an inhabitant occupier of that dwelling-house.

12. A person entitled to be registered as a parliamentary voter in respect of a lodger qualification—

Lodgers' qualification.

(*a*) must have claimed to be registered; and

(*b*) must have occupied separately as a lodger for the whole twelve months immediately preceding the fifteenth day of July next, lodgings, being part of one and the same dwelling-house in your parish [*or* township], and being of a clear yearly value, if let unfurnished, of ten pounds or upwards; and

(*c*) must have resided in such lodgings during the said twelve months.

If two or more persons are joint lodgers, and the value of the lodgings is such as to give ten pounds or more for each lodger, two of such persons but no more are entitled to be registered as parliamentary voters.

If a person has occupied different lodgings of the requisite value in the same house in immediate succession, he is

Precept by Clerk of Peace. entitled to be registered as a parliamentary voter in respect of the occupation thereof.

13. In addition to the Form B. which is required by paragraph 27 of my former precept to be published, you must, on or before the twentieth day of June next, publish in manner directed by paragraph 19 of my former precept, a notice signed by you according to the Form marked B. No. 2 among the printed forms sent herewith.

14. Form C. No. 1 sent herewith must be substituted for the Form C. No. 1 which I sent with my former precept, and which is required by paragraph 28 of my former precept to be served on or before the twentieth day of June.

22nd July. 15. If the sum due on account of poor rate or (if required) of county rate, in respect of any property is not paid on or before the twentieth day of July next, as required by the said notice, all occupiers of that property are disqualified from being entered in any list of county electors in respect of the old burgess qualification, or the ten pounds occupation-burgess qualification (as the case may be); and on or before the twenty-second of July next you are to add to the list mentioned in paragraph 29 of my former precept the name of every person so disqualified.

22nd July. 16. You are to ascertain, in accordance with paragraph 31 of my former precept, the names of all persons who are disqualified from being inserted in any list of county electors for your parish [*or* township] by reason of having received parochial relief.

17. The occupiers' list, which you were directed by paragraph 34 (*a*) of my former precept to make out on or before the last day of July next, in the Form E. sent with that precept, must include the names of all persons entitled

to be registered as county electors, and must be made out in three divisions in the Form E. sent herewith: **Precept by Clerk of Peace.**

Division 1 is to comprise the names of the persons entitled to be registered both as parliamentary occupation voters as defined in paragraphs 9 to 12 of this precept other than lodgers, and as county electors.

Division 2 is to comprise the names of the persons entitled to be registered as parliamentary occupation voters other than lodgers, but not as county electors.

Division 3 is to comprise the names of the persons entitled to be registered as county electors, but not as parliamentary occupation voters.

In Division 3 of such occupiers' list the nature of an old burgess qualification should be stated thus: "house," "warehouse," "counting-house," "chambers," or, as the case may be, with the addition of "joint" or "successive," if necessary.

18. You will also, on or before the last day of July next, make out a list in the form G. sent herewith, of all persons who, as mentioned in paragraph 6 of this precept, are entitled in respect of the occupation of property within your parish [*or* township] to be elected councillors of your county, but are not entitled to be on the county register thereof. 31st July.

Paragraph 37 and the subsequent paragraphs of my former precept will apply to this list as if it were one o the lists there mentioned, and you are to make out a separate objection list and claim list in relation to such list of persons entitled to be elected councillors, and deal with the same in manner directed by paragraphs 41 to 45 of my former precept respecting the occupiers' claim and objection lists.

Precept by Clerk of Peace.

19. Forms H., I., K., L., and M., among the printed forms sent herewith must be substituted for the forms H., I., K., L., and M., sent with my former precept.

If you fail to comply with this precept you will be liable to the penalties in that case provided.

Given under my hand this day of , 1888.

(Signed)

Clerk of the Peace for the County of

Application of Precept to Parish in small Municipal Borough.

Where a parish is in a municipal borough in which the lists of parliamentary voters are not made out under the Parliamentary and Municipal Registration Act of 1878, the supplemental precept and forms issued by the clerk of the peace to the overseers of that parish will be the same as the foregoing precept and forms, with the substitution, wherever necessary, of "burgess" for "county elector," of "municipal borough" for "county," and of "burgess roll" for "county register," and with the addition of the following paragraph:

25th Aug. On or before the twenty-fifth day of August next you are, besides delivering to me the documents mentioned in paragraph 45 of my former precept, to deliver to the town clerk of the municipal borough in which your parish [*or* township] is situate two copies of the occupiers' list and of the list required by paragraph 18 of this precept to be made out in the Form G. sent herewith, and a copy of each of the occupiers' claim and objection lists, made out and signed by you.

FORM OF SUPPLEMENTAL PRECEPT OF THE TOWN CLERK TO THE OVERSEERS IN THE YEAR 1888.

FORM B.—PARISHES WITHIN A PARLIAMENTARY BOROUGH, BUT NOT WITHIN A MUNICIPAL BOROUGH.

Registration of Parliamentary Voters and County Electors.

Parliamentary borough of
County of
to wit. } To the overseers of the poor of the parish of [*or* of the township of].

IN pursuance of the provisions of the County Electors Act, 1888, I require your attention to the following instructions respecting the registration of parliamentary voters and county electors.

This precept is supplemental to my former precept which I sent to you in April last.

---

1. In this precept the expression "county electors" means persons entitled to be registered in respect of the old burgess qualification or of the ten pounds occupation burgess qualification. **County electors.**

The expression "parliamentary voter" has the same meaning as in my former precept.

2. A county elector may be a man or a woman, but must be of full age and not subject to any legal incapacity, and must not at any time within the twelve months next before the fifteenth day of July next have received any parochial relief, but where a person has received for himself, or for any member of his family, any medical or surgical assist-

Precept by Town Clerk. ance, or any medicine, at the expense of any poor rate, he is not thereby deprived of his right to be registered.

Old burgess qualification.

3. A person entitled to be registered as a county elector in respect of the old burgess qualification—

(*a*) must during the whole of the twelve months immediately preceding the fifteenth day of July next have been an occupier of a house, warehouse, counting-house, shop, or other building in your parish [*or* township]; and

(*b*) have resided during those twelve months in the county or within seven miles thereof; and

(*c*) such person or some one else must during the said twelve months have been rated to all poor rates made in respect of the qualifying property; and

(*d*) all sums due in respect of the qualifying property on account of any poor rate made and allowed, during the twelve months immediately preceding the fifth day of January last, must have been paid on or before the twentieth day of July next; and

(*e*) if the county rate is not levied with the poor rate, all sums due in respect of the qualifying property on account of any county rate made during the twelve months immediately preceding the fifth day of January last, must have been paid on or before the twentieth day of July next.

A person is entitled to be registered in respect of the old burgess qualification notwithstanding that he has permitted his dwelling-house to be occupied as a furnished house for a time not exceeding four months, and during that time has not resided as above mentioned.

If two or more persons are joint occupiers of property qualifying for the old burgess qualification, each such occupier is entitled to be registered.

Precept by Town Clerk.

Ten pounds occupation burgess qualification.

4. A person entitled to be registered as a county elector in respect of the ten pounds occupation burgess qualification—

(*a*) must during the whole twelve months immediately preceding the fifteenth day of July have been an occupier as owner or tenant of some land or tenement in your parish [*or* township] of the clear yearly value of not less than ten pounds; and

(*b*) must have resided in or within seven miles of the said parliamentary borough during six months immediately preceding the fifteenth day of July next; and

(*c*) such person, or some one else, must during the said twelve months have been rated to all poor rates made in respect of such land or tenement; and

(*d*) all sums due in respect of the said land or tenement on account of any poor rate made and allowed during the twelve months immediately preceding the fifth day of January last, must have been paid on or before the twentieth day of July next.

If two or more persons jointly are such occupiers as above mentioned, and the value of the land or tenement is such as to give ten pounds or more for each occupier, each of such occupiers is entitled to be registered as a voter.

Succession.

5. If a person has occupied in immediate succession during the said twelve months different premises in the said parliamentary borough which would qualify him for registration as a county elector in respect of the old or ten pounds occupation burgess qualification, he is entitled, in respect of the occupation thereof, to be registered as a county elector in the parish [*or* township] in which the last occupied premises are situate.

Precept by Town Clerk.

Qualification of councillor. 5*a*. A person who is entitled to be registered as a county elector in all respects except that of residence, and is resident beyond seven miles, but within fifteen miles, of the said county, is entitled to be on the list of persons entitled to be elected councillors though not entitled to be on the county register.

20th June. 6. On or before the twentieth day of June next you are to publish, in manner directed by paragraph 19 of my former precept, a notice signed by you according to the Form B. No. 2 among the printed forms sent herewith.

20th June. 7. The notice which you are directed by paragraph 27 of any former precept to give on or before the twentieth day of June must be in Form C. No. 1 among the printed forms sent herewith, instead of the Form C. No. 1 previously sent.

22nd July. 8. If the sum due on account of poor rate or (if required) of county rate in respect of any property is not paid on or before the twentieth day of July next, as mentioned in the said notice, all occupiers of that property are disqualified from being entered in any list of county electors in respect of the old burgess qualification or the ten pounds occupation burgess qualification (as the case may be); and on or before the twenty-second of July next you are to add to the list mentioned in paragraph 28 of my former precept the name of every person so disqualified.

9. You are to ascertain, in accordance with paragraph 29 of my former precept, the names of all persons who are disqualified from being inserted in any list of county electors for your parish [*or* township] by reason of having received parochial relief.

31st July. 10. The occupiers' list which you are directed by paragraph 30, sub-paragraph (*a*), of my former precept to make out, must be made out in the Form D., No. 1, sent herewith, instead of in the form sent before, and must be made out in three divisions : **Precept by Town Clerk.**

Division one is to comprise the names of the persons entitled both to be registered as parliamentary voters in respect of a ten pounds occupation or household qualification and to be enrolled as county electors.

Division two is to comprise the names of the persons entitled to be registered as parliamentary voters in respect of a ten pounds occupation or household qualification, but not to be enrolled as county electors.

Division three is to comprise the names of the persons entitled to be enrolled as county electors, but not to be registered as parliamentary voters in respect of a ten pounds occupation or household qualification.

Where you are required to make out such occupiers' list according to the streets or the order in which the qualifying premises occur in the rate book, you will continue to make out the list in that manner.

In making out Division 3 of the occupiers' list, the nature of the old burgess qualification should be stated thus: "house," "warehouse," "counting-house," "chambers," or, as the case may be, with the addition of "joint," or "successive," if necessary.

11. You will also, on or before the last day of July next, make out a list in the Form G. sent herewith of all persons who, as mentioned in paragraph 6 of this precept, are entitled, in respect of the occupation of property within 31st July.

Precept by Town Clerk.

your parish [*or* township], to be elected councillors of your county, but are not entitled to be on the county register thereof.

Paragraph 31, and the subsequent paragraphs of my former precept, will apply to this list as if it were one of the lists there mentioned, and you are to make out a separate objection list and claim list in relation to such list of persons entitled to be elected councillors, and deal with the same in manner directed by paragraphs 35—39 of my former precept respecting the occupiers' claim and objection list.

12. Forms H., I., K., L., and M., among the printed forms sent herewith, must be substituted for the Forms H., I., K., L., and M., sent with my former precept.

If the officer issuing the precept is not the town clerk of a municipal borough, he should append to his signature his proper official description.

If you fail to comply with this precept, you will be liable to the penalties in that case provided.

Given under my hand this day of .

(Signed) *A.B.*,
Town Clerk of the Municipal Borough of .

FORM OF SUPPLEMENTAL PRECEPT OF THE TOWN CLERK TO THE OVERSEERS IN THE YEAR 1888.

Precept by Town Clerk.

FORM A.—PARISHES IN MUNICIPAL BOROUGHS WHERE THE LISTS ARE NOW MADE OUT UNDER THE PARLIAMENTARY AND MUNICIPAL REGISTRATION ACT OF 1878.

Enrolment of Burgesses.

Municipal borough of *to wit.* } To the overseers of the poor of the parish [*or* township] of

IN pursuance of the provisions of the County Electors Act, 1888, I require your attention to the following instructions respecting the enrolment of burgesses.

This precept is supplemental to my former precept which I sent to you in April last.

Additional burgess qualification.

1. Persons are entitled to be enrolled as burgesses in respect of the ten pounds occupation burgess qualification, as hereafter defined in paragraph 2 of this precept, as well as in respect of the old burgess qualification (that is to say, the qualification described in paragraph 8 of my former precept).

Ten pounds occupation burgess qualification.

2. A person entitled to be enrolled as a burgess in respect of the ten pounds occupation burgess qualification may be a man or woman, but must be of full age and not subject to any legal incapacity, and must not at any time within

Precept by Town Clerk.

the twelve months next before the fifteenth day of July next have received any parochial relief; but where a person has received for himself or for any member of his family any medical or surgical assistance, or any medicine at the expense of any poor rate, he is not thereby deprived of his right to be registered; and—

(*a*) must during the whole twelve months immediately preceding the fifteenth day of July next have been an occupier as owner or tenant of some land or tenement in your parish [*or* township] of the clear yearly value of not less than ten pounds; and

(*b*) must have resided in or within seven miles of the said municipal borough during six months immediately preceding the fifteenth day of July next; and

(*c*) such person or some one else must during the said twelve months have been rated to all poor rates made in respect of such land or tenement; and

(*d*) all sums due in respect of the said land or tenement on account of any poor rate made and allowed during the twelve months immediately preceding the fifth day of January last.

If two or more persons jointly are such occupiers as above mentioned, and the value of the land or tenement is such as to give ten pounds or more for each occupier, each of such occupiers is entitled to be registered as a voter.

If a person has occupied in the said municipal borough different lands or tenements of the requisite value in immediate succession during the said twelve months, he is entitled in respect of the occupation thereof to be registered as a voter in the parish [*or* township] in which the last occupied land or tenement is situate.

Precept by Town Clerk.

Qualification of councillors.

3. A person who is entitled to be registered as a burgess in respect of the ten pounds occupation burgess qualification in all respects except that of residence, and is resident beyond seven miles, but within fifteen miles, of the said municipal borough, is entitled to be on the list of persons mentioned in sub-paragraph (*d*) of paragraph 30 of my former precept as entitled to be elected councillors or aldermen though not entitled to be on the burgess roll.

20th June.

4. Form B., No. 2, sent herewith must be substituted for the Form B., No. 2, which I sent before, and which is required by paragraph 26 of my former precept to be published on or before the twentieth of June.

20th June.

Form C., No. 1, sent herewith must be substituted for Form C., No. 1, sent with my former precept, and required by paragraph 27 of my former precept to be served on or before the twentieth of June.

If you fail to comply with this precept you will be liable to the penalties in that case provided.

Given under my hand this day of .

(Signed) *A.B.*,

Town Clerk of the Municipal Borough of .

INDEX.

London: Printed by Shaw & Sons, Fetter Lane & Crane Court, E.C.